Collins · *do brilliantly !*

Includes To

Mind

Exam**Practice**

GCSE English

Exam practice at its **best**

John Reynolds
Series Editor: Jayne de Courcy

William Collins' dream of knowledge for all began with the publication of his first book in 1819.
A self-educated mill worker, he not only enriched millions of lives, but also founded a flourishing publishing house.
Today, staying true to this spirit, Collins books are packed with inspiration, innovation and practical expertise.
They place you at the centre of a world of possibility and give you exactly what you need to explore it.

Collins. Do more.

Published by Collins
An imprint of HarperCollins*Publishers*
77–85 Fulham Palace Road
Hammersmith
London
W6 8JB

Browse the complete Collins catalogue at
www.collinseducation.com

First published 2001
This revised edition published 2005

10 9 8 7 6 5 4 3 2

ISBN-13 978 0 00 721546 1
ISBN-10 0 00 721546 0

John Reynolds asserts the moral right to be identified as the author of this work.

British Library Cataloguing in Publication Data
A Catalogue record for this publication is available from the British Library.

Acknowledgements
The Author and Publishers are grateful to the following for permission to reproduce copyright material:
Cadogan Holidays The Award Winning Tour Operator (tel. 023 80 828313) for the extract from their Cadogan Holiday Morocco Brochure, October 2002–2003 (p 36); Curtis Brown for the poem 'Island Man' by Grace Nichols (p 45); Heinemann Educational for the poems 'Blessing' by Imtiaz Dharker (p 46), 'The Lake Isle of Innisfree' by William Butler Yeats, with permission of AP Watts Limited (p 51) and 'Vultures' by Chinua Achebe (pp 89–90); Kasbah for the extract from their website **www.kasbah.com** (p 37); MacMillan, London, UK for the extract from *Is that it?* by Bob Geldof (p 12); Oxford University Press India, New Delhi for the poem 'Night of the Scorpion' by Nissim Ezekiel (pp 87–88); © Susan Riley/Mizz/IPC Syndication for the article 'Bouncing back' (pp 28–29); *The Guardian* for John Ezard's account of a tornado (pp 16–17); *The Mail on Sunday* for the articles 'Nightmare of the Grey Goo' by Jonathan Oliver (p 84), 'Tiny robots with massive potential' (p 85) and 'Who will control the nanobots?' by Jonathon Porritt (p 86); *The Times*, London, © NI Syndication, London (20 January 1997) for the article called 'Whose history essay is it anyway?' by Joe Joseph (pp 22–23); Weidenfeld & Nicolson for the extract from *Sahara* by Michael Palin (pp 35–36); also to the following exam board for permission to reproduce GCSE questions: OCR (pp 59 and 94).

Photographs
Andrew Syred/SPL (p 84); Cadogan Holidays The Award Winning Tour Operator (p 36); Eye of Science/SPL (p 86); José Luis Pelaez, Inc./CORBIS (p 23); © Mizz/IPC Syndication (p 28).

Every effort has been made to contact the holders of copyright material, but if any have been inadvertently overlooked, the Publishers will be pleased to make the necessary arrangements at the first opportunity.

Edited by Jenny Draine and Neil Morris
Mind Maps artwork by Kathy Baxendale
Production by Katie Butler
Book design by Bob Vickers
Printed and bound by Printing Express, Hong Kong

Contents

How this book will help you by John Reynolds

This book takes you through the different kinds of Reading and Writing questions you will come across in your English exam papers. It helps you **identify key words in questions and revise key skills in answering questions.** It makes clear what examiners look for in answers in order to award them high marks.

Reading through this book as part of your revision will **help you with your exam technique and give you the best possible chance of achieving a high grade in your exam.**

The first seven chapters in this book are broken down into five elements aimed at giving you as much guidance as possible:

1 Typical exam questions

Each chapter contains **two typical exam questions.** For Reading, these are usually part questions, so that they don't take up too much space. For Writing, they are usually complete questions. **I have emphasised and commented on the key words in these questions.** This should help you to understand clearly what is required by the questions which you meet in your exam. So often students lose marks in their exam because they misread or misinterpret the questions.

2 Extracts from students' answers at Grade C and Grade A

I have included **Grade C** answers to some questions. **I highlight the good points and then show how you could improve them.** I have also included **Grade A** answers. Here **I make clear what makes these such good answers so that you can try to demonstrate similar skills in your own exam answers.** In some cases I have used **extracts** rather than complete answers so that you can immediately see the points which are being made and don't have too much to read!

3 'Don't forget...' boxes

These boxes highlight **all the really important things you need to remember** when tackling a particular type of Reading or Writing question in your exam. You might like to read these boxes through the night before your exam as a 'quick check' on what to do to score high marks.

4 Key skill

This section focuses on a **key Reading or Writing skill.** I have written it as **a series of easy-to-remember bullet points** so that you can simply and quickly revise what you have learnt during your English course.

5 What the examiners are looking for

This page tells you as clearly as possible what an examiner expects from an answer in order to award it a Grade C or a Grade A. **This should help you to demonstrate 'high scoring' skills in your answers to exam questions.**

6 Practice questions, answers and examiner's comments

Chapters 8 and 9 contain sample Reading and Writing exam questions. These questions are for you to try answering once you have read through the earlier chapters.

Hints on exam technique

Reading

Before you start

- Although you will have been told what to do by your teacher, **read all the instructions on the exam paper carefully**. This includes reading those on the front page as well.

- Make sure that you know how many questions you should answer in each section. Check whether there are choices within questions; it's not unknown for candidates to lose concentration and answer more questions than they need to!

- **Work out how much time you need to spend on each question**. The marks available will be printed after every question; make sure that you use this information to help you divide up your time: you should spend twice as much time on a 20 mark question than you should on one worth only 10 marks, for example.

- **Check very carefully which reading passages apply to which questions**. Avoid introducing material from the wrong passage, as this will be ignored by the examiner as irrelevant.

- **Read through and think about all the questions on the paper before you start your first answer**. If you know what the questions are about, part of your brain can be thinking about those to come even while you're answering a different one.

- Remember: **you do not have to answer the questions in the order in which they are printed on the exam paper**. However, you should make it clear to the examiner which question you are answering by writing the number in the margin. This is particularly important when there is a choice of writing tasks on a similar topic.

Questions on non-fiction and media texts

- Make sure that you read the questions carefully as well as the passages. Keep the questions firmly in mind as you read the passages and try to identify material which is directly related to answering them.

- Make sure that you highlight or underline relevant sections of the reading material.

- Read actively; think of the questions your teacher would ask to prompt the right response to comprehension work in lessons and ask yourself (and answer) those questions.

- If the question contains bullet points or mentions specific topics, use these as a backbone for your answer.

- Remember that with reading questions you should spend much of your time doing exactly that. You must understand what you are reading as fully as possible before you start to write.

- Especially with longer tasks, plan your answer by making notes from which you can produce a fair version. In particular, decide what your overall approach is going to be and how you are going to conclude your response. Make sure that the points you make illustrate and support this.

- Remember that it is your responsibility to convince the examiner that you have understood what you have read; the best way to do this is to express your answer by using your own words and not by just copying words and phrases from the reading material.

- If you use quotations to support a comment, make sure that these are the best you can choose for your purpose and remember to explain how they illustrate your point.

- When you are answering questions about the way writers use language, remember that there is no one right answer; think about the writer's choice of vocabulary and the associations of the words used and then explain the effect they have on you.

- When you have finished answering the questions, check your answers carefully. In particular, make sure that there is nothing which could mislead or confuse an examiner in your spelling and punctuation.

- Check that you have made clear how your comments relate directly to the question you are answering.

How to avoid common mistakes

- Spend sufficient time reading the question and the passages. Too many candidates produce incomplete answers by starting to write before they have a full understanding of what they are reading.

- Take careful note of the wording of the question. Distinguish carefully in your answer between questions which contain the word 'what?' and those which contain the word 'how?' The latter will expect you to analyse and comment. Make sure you do this in a precise and focused way; vague generalisations will not impress an examiner.

Writing

General points

In any writing that you do under exam conditions, remember the following:

- Spend some time **thinking about and planning what you are going to write**. Don't produce too elaborate a plan, however; a spider diagram or a list of paragraph topic sentences is sufficient as long as you have given thought to how to structure your writing.

- In particular, think carefully about your **opening and closing paragraphs**. Always have a clear idea of how you are going to end your writing; this helps to focus the rest of the plan.

- You only have one chance when writing essays under exam conditions; it is important that you **involve your audience** with your opening paragraph and leave them with a lasting impression through your conclusion.

- Keep thinking about **audience, register and the reader**. The task may give you a specific audience (e.g. your fellow students) and register (e.g. to write the words of a speech). However, your reader is also the examiner. Make sure that your writing can be easily read and that you take care over accuracy. Any slips of expression which prevent the examiner from gaining a clear understanding of what you mean to say are likely to reduce your potential mark.

- Try to write with some **variation of sentence types**; you need to show the examiner that you are able to **control complex structures** and use **interesting vocabulary**. You cannot be rewarded for something you haven't done.

- Remember the basics: the **correct use of full stops, paragraphs and apostrophes** could make the difference between success and failure.

- It is likely that the task will have a suggested word limit; there is no merit in exceeding this. The more you write, the greater the chance of making careless slips of expression.

- Finally, don't forget that this is an examination which tests your skills in reading and writing English; it is not a test of your creative abilities so don't spend too long agonising over how original and imaginative your ideas are. What you write must be **relevant and appropriate**, but usually it is the **quality of your expression** which counts.

Writing tasks to inform, explain, describe

You need to concentrate on:

- **purpose**: what information, explanation or description are you being asked to give and why are you being asked to give it?

- **audience**: for whom is what you are writing intended? Remember to select a register and vocabulary suited to the audience and purpose.

- **focus**: what you write should give clear information or advice. You are being asked to communicate specific details; it is, therefore, a good idea to write in an appropriate tone without too many verbal pyrotechnics.

Writing tasks to argue, persuade, advise

You need to concentrate on:

- the **type of task and the viewpoint**. Are you going to adopt a balanced tone, weighing both sides of an argument, or make a powerful, rhetorical statement to influence your audience into sharing your opinions?

- the **language** you use. Will you try to convince by using rational, objective vocabulary and controlled sentence structures, or will you employ emotive language and forceful rhetorical questions? Whatever you decide on, remember – be consistent.

- supporting your argument with **evidence and examples** and ensuring that you make effective use of them.

Writing tasks to analyse, review, comment

You need to concentrate on:

- how best to use any **stimulus material** given on the question paper: will you stay close to it, adapt it for your own purposes or ignore it altogether?

- the **examples and evidence** you are going to use. You must refer to things about which you have sufficient knowledge or experience to make convincingly developed comments.

- the **approach** you are going to take. You should adopt an **objective tone**, but it helps to base your comments on an analysis of how you react to your chosen topic.

How to avoid common mistakes

- **Keep focused on the task** and remember the time constraints; don't try to be over-ambitious and try to write too much.

- In general, keep what you write based in your own experience; writing well under exam conditions is difficult enough without the added complications of creating imaginary worlds or situations.

- Remember the **audience and purpose** of your writing and make sure that you use an **appropriate register** for the task.

- Show that you are **in control of the language you use** by using a wide range of vocabulary and grammatical structures. Don't be afraid of using sophisticated vocabulary just because you are uncertain of how to spell some words; you'll still be given credit for knowing them and using them correctly.

Why MIND MAPS® will help you

by TONY BUZAN

Mind Maps really are a shortcut to exam success. They can help you to plan your revision, to organise your work and to remember important information in your exams.

What is a Mind Map?

First of all, a Mind Map is a way of organising your thoughts. Then, because you have created it yourself, and used colours and pictures to make it 'stick' in your brain, it is a way of helping you to remember those thoughts.

A Mind Map is like exercise for your brain. The shapes, colours and pictures on your Mind Map keep your brain active and help you to remember the important facts and ideas.

How do I create a Mind Map?

The Mind Map below shows you some of the important rules to follow. It is an essay plan based on the typical exam question in Chapter 7:

'Popular TV programmes reflect real life and help the viewers to understand the world of which they are part.'

Analyse this statement and, by referring to one or two TV programmes, comment on how far you think it can be justified.

Here's how you do it:

- Start with paper and lots of coloured pens.
- Turn the paper sideways and write the main focus of your answer in the middle of the paper.

Add a drawing to help you remember. You don't have to be a great artist: the important thing here is to keep things lively and colourful.

- Now let your imagination get to work! Draw 4 or 5 branches from the central idea for each of the main topics. Write the key word for that topic on the branch, filling up the length of the branch.
- Then you can add smaller branches as you think of how each main topic can break down further. Use only one word for each idea.
- Use a different colour for each main branch and its sub-branches. Colour adds fun and will help you remember.
- Illustrate the branches with small pictures, shapes and colours.
- You can use arrows, underlining or boxes, to link ideas on different branches.

Planning essays

You can use Mind Maps to help plan all your essay answers. So why not start another Mind Map with one of the GCSE questions from this book at the centre of the paper? Then add in all the things that make a good answer for that type of question.

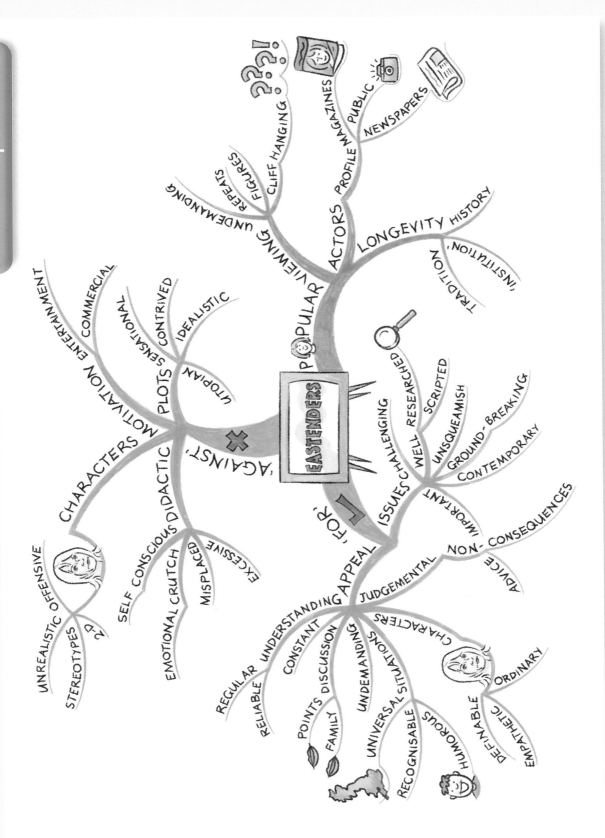

Typical exam question

Read carefully Bob Geldof's account of his meeting with Mother Theresa. What do you learn about her appearance and character and how does the writer convey her special qualities?

Refer closely to the content and the language of the passage in your answer. Use your own words as far as possible. [20 marks]

We were sitting in the departure lounge when Mother Theresa came in with several other nuns all wearing the white habits with blue borders of the Sisters of Charity. She was astonishingly tiny. When I went to greet her I found that I towered more than two feet above her. She was a battered, wizened woman. The thing that struck me most forcibly was her feet. Her habit was clean and well-cared for but her sandals were beaten up pieces of leather from which her feet protruded, gnarled and misshapen as old tree roots.

I bent to kiss her. I do not normally kiss strangers on a first meeting but it seemed like the right thing to do. She bowed her head swiftly so that I was obliged to kiss the top of her wimple. It disturbed me. I found out later she only let lepers kiss her. The photographers crowded round. We sat down. I felt like a clumsy giant next to her. I showed her my shoes which were beginning to fall apart and asked her if she had any spare sandals. She laughed. Actually she cackled out loud. I gave her a copy of the record. I could not think what else to do. I'm sure she got rid of it as soon as she was on the plane for Calcutta. Then she began to tell me about her work in Ethiopia. Her nuns were working in the shanty towns of the capital and they also ran a feeding centre and hospital at Alomata in the famine-stricken province of Wollo where they cared for the old, the blind, the disabled and the incurably ill – the people tragically overlooked by the other agencies who concentrated on trying to save the children, the pregnant and mothers of the very young. It was the same philosophy she adopts in India. I told her that my band had played in India and that, if it seemed a good idea, next time we were there we would do a benefit concert for her mission. She said that she didn't need fund-raising activities – God would provide. She then gave a clear demonstration of the way in which God provided.

While the TV cameras were rolling she turned to Commissioner Dawit Wolde Georgis, the head of the RRC, and said that on the way to the airport she had seen a couple of old palaces which she had been told were empty and she asked him if she could have them as homes for orphans. With the cameras whirring Dawit did a bit of fancy footwork. 'Well, I'm not sure about those particular places. I don't know what they're being used for. But…er…I'm sure we can find you some suitable premises for an orphanage…'

'Two orphanages,' she corrected.

'Two orphanages,' he conceded.

Is That It? by Bob Geldof

What are the key words in this question?

- **Read carefully** This tells you that the examiners will be expecting a response which contains specific **details** taken from the passage. A generalised response will not gain a high grade.

- **What do you learn** This tells you that you must use facts from the passage.

- **Appearance and character** There are **two** points to look for; the first may seem straightforward but it is important not to ignore it.

- **How does the writer convey** You have to write about the way the writer uses language; use quotations from the passage and then explain how they work.

- **Special qualities** There are specific points to look for in terms of what makes Mother Theresa a special person. Remember, some of these are likely to be **implied** rather than openly stated. Answers that search out and explain **inferences** always gain high marks.

- **Use your own words** You need to show the examiner that you have clearly understood the material you have been reading. Using your own words will help to do this.

Penny's Grade **C** answer

Mother Theresa is a very tiny woman. She has other nuns with her who wear white habits with blue borders. She has gnarled and twisted feet and wears sandals. Although her clothes are clean, the way that her sandals are described suggests that she doesn't worry very much about what she looks like. She is obviously concerned about more important things.

She doesn't like people to kiss her apart from lepers. She seems to be a happy person because she cackles when she laughs. She is obviously a very good person because she works in very poor areas helping the disabled and very ill. She has a very strong belief in God and thinks that he will always help to provide what she wants. She seems to be quite used to appearing on television.

GOOD POINTS

Penny's response just makes it into Grade C for the following reasons:

CONTENT: There is a sound understanding of the more straightforward points of the passage but they are explained in a rather superficial way.

COMMENT: The comments at the end of the first paragraph show that Penny has some insight into Mother Theresa's character and this is supported by direct reference to the passage.

UNDERSTANDING: The final sentence indicates that Penny has some appreciation of inference (what is not directly stated) but the comment is not developed or explained fully enough.

IMPROVEMENTS NEEDED

▶ The answer needs more detailed explanation; it contains mainly descriptive statements.

▶ It would benefit from greater use of quotations and some more specific references.

▶ Penny has selectively lifted words and phrases from the original passage. She needs to use her own words more to show the examiner that she has genuinely understood the meaning of what she has read.

▶ She needs to read beneath the surface of the text to pull out some of Mother Theresa's special qualities that are implied rather than directly stated.

Mark's Grade **A** answer

This answer takes account of the points made above.

Mother Theresa is very small – the writer tells us how he "towered more than two feet above her". She is very old and the skin on her face is shrivelled up. She is dressed in a nun's costume which is white with blue borders. The writer was most struck by her feet: she was wearing battered old sandals and her feet were twisted and out of shape. This would suggest that she spends a lot of time walking on them; the description of them as being like "old tree roots" also suggests strength and durability.

Mother Theresa seems to be a woman of very strong principles. Although Bob Geldof is a famous person, she does not allow him to kiss her face as she only allows lepers to kiss her. This shows that she is highly principled and very humble as she doesn't make exceptions or concessions for anybody. She obviously has a sense of humour as she laughs when the writer asks her if she has any spare sandals. Her laugh is, rather surprisingly, described as a "cackle" and this makes her seem more like an ordinary human being and a not entirely respectable one at that. She is obviously very much part of the world about her.

We learn about her charity work, both in Ethiopia and India. The fact that she begins to talk about it almost straightaway shows how important it is to her; she obviously devotes her life to caring for the very sick and needy. Her principles and spirituality are also clear when she mentions that she does not need fund-raising activities, however, as God will provide.

Bob Geldof suggests that Mother Theresa is much more practical than she might appear on the surface and this is what enables her to get what she wants. When she is taking part in a live television discussion with Commissioner Georgis, she very skilfully manipulates the situation to make it very difficult for him to refuse her request for premises for two orphanages. The terse way in which this is described: "'Two orphanages,' she corrected. 'Two orphanages,' he conceded," illustrates how effectively she succeeded in getting what she wanted.

What makes this a good answer?

► Mark's answer shows an excellent **overall grasp** both of what the question is asking for and what the passage is about.

► Mark uses his own words to show that he understands what he has read and **the material is well organised into paragraphs**.

► Mark gives many **precise details** about Mother Theresa's appearance. He shows he has a good appreciation of Bob Geldof's opinion of her character and the way in which Geldof uses language to convey this.

► Mark has drawn **several inferences** from the passage about her special qualities. In particular, he expresses clearly the way that the television interview reveals a strongly practical streak beneath her spirituality; and he interprets the reference to her 'cackle' as an indication that there is much about Mother Theresa that is very down-to-earth despite her very spiritual life.

Typical exam question

Read carefully John Ezard's account of the effects of a tornado on Oklahoma.

- **What facts have you learnt about the tornado and its effects?**
- **Explain and comment on the writer's thoughts and opinions about what happened.**

[20 marks]

Travel writer John Ezard was in Oklahoma during a tornado. Here is his reaction.

Oklahoma is a highly distinctive American state; and that shows in the reaction of its people to their spasmodic catastrophes. Three years ago when 168 men and women were killed in the state capital's worst single disaster, the bombing of the Alfred Murragh federal headquarters, staff in the city's largest tower block arranged their office lighting so that it projected the sign of the cross. Yesterday morning, as they commuted to work past the confetti-like debris of more than 7,000 homes in the suburbs of Mid West City and Moore City, they did something rare on any freeway and almost unprecedented here. They slowed their cars down to 15 miles per hour.

Mostly it wasn't to gawp because you couldn't see much detail past the police barriers and the tall walls of the highways. It was a mark of respect, almost of reverence, for the ending of 38 lives and, temporarily at least, of the proud, earnest material dreams of thousands more families. The passers-by turned their vehicles into an impromptu, collective, funeral cortege. It might so easily have happened to them, the series of vortexes that sucked humans and the fabric or their lives towards the sky and spat them back to earth in these aspiring middle-class satellite townships within a few seconds. At dawn yesterday, which broke with a clear sunny sky after the torrential thunder storms and continuing statewide tornado alerts of Tuesday, you could for the first time realise what had struck these new model Main Streets.

Sound brick houses, built around traditional timber frames, have been at best left looking like shanty town remnants and at worst like Dresden after the fire storm. You can still see what neat places Moore and Mid West used to be. Now they are flimsy death traps which need bulldozing. Yesterday afternoon thousands of survivors were allowed back for a strictly limited two hours to fumble through the ruins of Mid West City and salvage possessions by the car load. They are desperate to retrieve not only their family photos and videos and their children's clothes but their TVs and microwaves. These possessions had to be saved for, or paid off by credit card, and if you can recover them then rebuilding your life is a mite easier. 'First nature shatters my life. Now the government is going to bury my possessions,' said one frantic woman, her face still blood-flecked with cuts from the flying debris.

In time the dead will get their public memorials, like the one which is due to be opened next year to the Murragh bomb victims. Here, the bomb is seen as an incomprehensible atrocity from another planet, an event to be buried deep in memory. But the twisters come every year, their spouts grubbing up and spewing out soil, property and sometimes people, like giant malignant earthworms reaching down from the sky. Moore City had its last tornado as recently as October.

Moving at 35 miles an hour, engorged with sucked-up debris, this evil killer grew to a base more than a quarter of a mile broad which started to twinkle with grey flashes as it brought down power lines. 'My God. This thing is a monster,' said a TV weather man. Then another twister developed nearby and they marched together like twin Hiroshima mushroom clouds. 'God, it just hit. It was so loud, much louder than last time,' Ronna Johnson said. 'Our house was covered with mud. And then I started crying. I said, "This is not right..."'

Within minutes the response was as practised and organised as in a disturbed anthill. Neighbours trained in mouth-to-mouth resuscitation were sought to treat the heart victims that twisters always cause. Six designated emergency hostels were re-opened, and within an hour Wayland Bonds, Moore's schools superintendent, who lost two schools and a technology centre, was planning how to complete the school year without them. Less than two days afterwards, the event is beginning to lose its grip on public interest. Last night, even on local radio bulletins, the topic of tornado damage had dropped to third place. And during the commercial breaks – 'in this difficult time' – the Prudential Insurance Company was urging prudent people to take out policies to protect those material dreams during the next big blow.

What are the key words in this question?

- The first key word here is *what*. The first part of the question asks you to identify information contained in the passage. Notice, however, that you are asked to identify only *facts* related to the tornado and its effects, not **opinions**.

- The second part of the question asks you to *explain and comment on* the writer's *thoughts and opinions*. Here you need to identify the writer's personal response to the tornado, the language he uses to convey this, and the effect he is trying to create on the reader.

Sophie's Grade **A** answer

The tornadoes struck Mid West City and Moore City in Oklahoma on a Tuesday. Over 7000 homes, mainly in prosperous middle-class areas, were demolished. Many of these were solidly built brick and timber houses and this shows the force of the storm. Even houses that remained standing were covered in mud. In total, 38 people were killed and the lives of the survivors were wrecked as they had lost so much personal property. Power lines, schools and factories were destroyed. Although tornadoes are an annual event in this part of America (and this is shown by the trained and organised response of the people to the disaster, particularly towards helping those suffering from heart problems), this particular one seemed to be exceptional. The base of the tornado was more than a quarter of a mile wide and it was joined by a second tornado; together they produced an extremely loud noise. These are the facts contained in the passage.

In general, the writer's thoughts and opinions about the tornado and its effects concern his sympathy and respect for the people who suffered it and his impression of the tornado itself as a terrifying, unnatural monster.

His respect for the people of Oklahoma is shown by his description of it as a "highly distinctive American state" and his account of the way in which its inhabitants took part in the "rare and unprecedented" gesture of slowing down their cars on the freeway as a mark of respect to the victims.

The language which is used to personify the tornado ("sucked humans and the fabric of their lives towards the sky and spat them back to earth") shows his sympathy for the victims and how he regards the tornado as a heartless monster which feeds off humans and discards them when it has had enough.

The writer seems to be critical of officialdom. He includes a quote from one victim complaining that "the government is going to bury my possessions". This makes the government seem heartless in its rush to clear up the mess before everyone has a chance to salvage what can be recovered.

The writer further represents the twisters as inhuman, terrifying monsters "grubbing up...spewing out...giant malignant earthworms...evil killer". The reference to the mushroom clouds at Hiroshima (where atomic bombs came out of a clear sky and destroyed a city) emphasises the destructiveness of the storm and its unfairness to innocent people.

The concluding paragraph shows that the writer feels the outside world has a very short memory when it comes to other people's problems. He uses irony to highlight the cynicism of the insurance company that wants to cash in "in this difficult time" by "urging prudent people" to protect their "material dreams" against "the next big blow".

What makes this a good answer?

▶ There is clear evidence that Sophie is **aware of the difference between fact and opinion**. She makes a point of showing this by dealing with the two parts of the question in separate paragraphs.

▶ The facts relating to the tornado and its effects are **identified and expressed in Sophie's own words**. They are well-organised and do not slavishly follow the order of the original passage. In this way it is clear to the examiner that the candidate has a thorough understanding of the passage.

▶ When dealing with the writer's opinions and thoughts, Sophie shows she is able to **infer** what the writer thinks and feels from the language that he uses. Not only does Sophie **quote** appropriate examples from the original article, but she also **explains how these selected quotations illustrate the point being made** – so making it easy for the examiner to credit the points made.

Key skills

These are the skills which exam questions on non-fiction texts set out to test:

1

Your ability to distinguish between fact and opinion and to evaluate the ways in which information is presented.

Remember: a fact is something which can be proved to be true; an opinion is what someone thinks about something but the truth of which cannot be proved. ('Apples grow on trees' is a fact; 'Apples taste disgusting' is an opinion.)

2

Your ability to follow an argument.

For example, you may be asked to show that you can do this by expressing something you have read in your own words or by writing an argument against the original to show that you have understood its main points.

3

The ability to show an understanding of the ways writers use language, structure and presentation to convey their information.

This involves analysing and explaining **how** these different devices are used, taking examples from the passage you have read and commenting on them in detail.

DON'T FORGET ...

✓ You need to make clear to the examiner how well you have understood the question; the examiner cannot award marks for points you haven't made. **Don't assume that some points are so obvious that they are not worth mentioning**; unless you show that you are aware of them, the examiner cannot reward you for knowing them.

✓ It is the ability to identify and explain points which are **implied** in what you read which allows you to achieve top grades.

✓ An understanding of **tone** and **register** and how well they are suited to the chosen **audience** will help in an analysis of the writer's techniques.

✓ **Keep focused on the question** at all times in your answer. Do not include irrelevant personal opinions or comments.

✓ It is your responsibility to make your understanding clear. One way of doing this is by **using your own words** whenever possible. (You will not be expected to reword technical vocabulary, however.)

✓ Another way of showing your understanding is by **reorganising information** from the original passage to match the requirements of the question.

What the examiners are looking for

To achieve a Grade C when writing about non-fiction texts you should:

1 Show a sound understanding of what you have read.

In particular, you should be able to show a good grasp of the straightforward points contained in the original.

2 Select appropriate details from the passage which are relevant to the question.

3 Give evidence that the meaning of the passage has been understood.

You can show this by making an attempt to use your own words.

4 Select some references and quotations when writing about the writer's techniques and make some attempt to explain how they are used.

To achieve a Grade A when writing about non-fiction texts you should:

1 Ensure that your answer is fully focused on the question.
There should be no irrelevance or padding.

2 Show that you have a complete understanding of the material.
A consistent use of own words is a good way to give evidence of this and so is rearranging the original material in order to focus directly on the question.

3 Refer to a wide range of appropriate points taken from the original.

4 Give clear evidence that inferences have been clearly understood.

5 Adopt a consistently analytical approach when writing about the writer's techniques.

6 Give detailed references to and relevant quotations from the original to back up original insights and comments that you make.

Read closely the newspaper article _Whose history essay is it anyway?_

What impression does it give of the way homework is viewed by the writer? In your answer you should comment on:

- **the presentation**
- **the content**
- **the use of language.**

[20 marks]

Whose history essay is it anyway?

THE current generation of homework-doers is fraying from the strain of overwork. Just when they've got home in the evenings and ache to slump in front of _The Simpsons_ on TV they have to buckle down to a page of algebra or an essay on Anne Boleyn – although we parents wouldn't mind doing all this extra work if our children showed more gratitude now and then.

Of course, teachers don't actually send home a note saying: 'Dear Parent, draw a cross-section of a leaf cell in your child's biology book.' But sensitive parents feel under great emotional pressure to help out, because they don't want their child to be ridiculed in class the next day by children whose neat leaf-cell diagrams prove that they have made far greater progress in the important educational discipline of blackmailing their parents into doing their homework.

'In the real world there is no such thing as a fraction'

The pressure – if not the responsibility – to make sure that homework gets done falls on parents, which is dispiriting because their heart just isn't in it any longer. If adults once knew why it might have been important to know how to address a table in Latin, then they have certainly forgotten now.

And it's difficult to appear convincing when you tell a seven-year-old that it's crucial to learn the exact length of the Nile, when you know that the exact length of the Nile is a statistic that has proved to be of as much practical value in adult life as knowing which side of the bed the Prime Minister prefers to sleep on. If you ever get around to taking a holiday in Egypt, you can always just look up the figure in a travel guide.

An adult's eyes glaze over at the sight of fractions. Who cares what seven twelfths divided by two fifths is? Adults know that in the real world there is no such thing as a fraction, at least not for anything an adult might crave: you can't have four fifths of an Aston Martin, or one third of a roulette chip. In the real world knowing fractions is a lot less useful than knowing the name of an accountant who has a spirit of adventure when it comes to tax returns.

There _are_ ways of passing the homework buck. One popular option in parts of

Hampstead was to hire clever Yugoslav *au pairs* who had fled their homeland and universities when Yugoslavia crumbled: to them, your child's maths homework was a doddle. One downside of peace in the area (Yugoslavia, not Hampstead) is that the supply of these smart *au pairs* has shrivelled.

Another is to slip your children some money and pack them off to an Internet café where they post their A-Level physics homework into cyberspace and wait for show-offs to file back the solutions: an insider advises plumping for German respondents, who are more concise than Americans, which means there is less to download.

The increasing reliance by school examiners on coursework (much of it done at home) for a pupil's end-of-year exam marks has only swelled the emotional pressure on parents. In the old days, if their children failed their exams you could blame *them* – if only they had revised a bit harder!

But now it is the parents who feel guilty. 'Maybe I should have gone to the National Portrait Gallery and bought postcards of Henry VIII's six wives for the history coursework,' they chastise themselves. Not that you can just glue them onto a sheet of A4 any more. Home computers with desktop publishing programs mean that every parent can be enough of a typographer and dust jacket designer to make their children's project really stand out from the rest of the dossiers handed in to the teacher.

The increasing reliance by examiners on coursework (much of it done at home) has only swelled the emotional pressure on parents

Many parents worry that their children might be genetically programmed to find homework irksome, but a visit to a Harley Street specialist will show that there is often a simple treatment for this – known as 'monetary bribes'. Some parents console themselves with the knowledge that Solomon, Chaucer and Shakespeare never did a jot of homework whereas Roy Keane, Kylie Minogue and Gareth Gates did. Discuss.

Other parents like to try out the latest tricks to make homework palatable. A teacher in a Los Angeles school decided to teach maths in an argot more in tune with the rhythms of his pupils' lives and resorted to rap, such as: 'Six times seven is 42, Babe I wanna make love to you.' Try this at home: 'Henry VIII he did not grieve, when he divorced Anne of Cleves.' Still making no progress? What about: 'Write your piece on Paul Revere, or I'll clip you round the ear.'

By Joe Joseph for *The Times*, London, 20 January 1997

What are the key words in this question?

● *Read closely*   Close reading is a key skill. You should spend at least 10 minutes reading the passage and gaining as full an understanding of it as you can. Keep the question at the front of your mind as you read and ask yourself questions to ensure that you can see how the main issues can be answered.

● *Impression*   This means that you should attempt to show an understanding of what you think the writer's purpose is and how effectively it has been passed on to the reader (that is, *you*).

● *Presentation*   In general, this refers to the way the writing is presented on the page (the use of columns, photographs, headlines, etc.).

However, it also implies that there should be some consideration of the way the writer has presented his argument.

● *Content*   This refers to the examples and other points which the writer uses to interest the reader. Does the passage contain facts, opinions or a mixture of both?

● *Use of language*   This is an argumentative piece of writing. How does the writer use language to get you to share his point of view? You should consider the **vocabulary** he uses and the **implications** of particular words and phrases. **Identifying and explaining the writer's tone of voice (register)** is also important.

Jason's Grade C answer

The article is set out in columns and is clearly from a newspaper. There is a photograph of a rather bored looking boy trying to do his homework and his thoughts are shown in a bubble. It's quite a large picture and will attract the reader's attention. It might make readers think of their own school days and how they found homework boring too. There's also a quotation in the middle of the page which says "In the real world there's no such thing as a fraction." This also suggests that the writer is not very much in favour of homework.

The writer makes quite a lot of jokes in the article because he talks about parents doing homework for children as if it's something they're expected to do. He says what they really want to do is watch "The Simpsons" instead like a lot of children do. He then goes

GOOD POINTS

Jason's answer is a sound C Grade for the following reasons:

UNDERSTANDING: There is quite a good understanding of the presentation of the article and some relevant comments which attempt to explain how the presentation conveys the writer's feelings. The final sentence of the first paragraph also indicates a sound understanding of the writer's point of view.

REFERENCES: There are some appropriate references to the content of the article and some relevant details have been identified.

LANGUAGE: Although the comments about the writer's use of language tend to be descriptive, the final point, which shows an understanding of the writer's tone, is sufficient to confirm this as a secure C Grade response.

on to talk about a lot of things which teachers expect you to learn, like the length of the Nile, which are of no use in real life. Then he talks about ways in which parents can get out of doing homework by sending their children off to an internet cafe so that they can find out the answers and says that old-fashioned famous people like Shakespeare never did homework but modern people like Roy Keane and Kylie Minogue did and that would seem to suggest that homework is a waste of time.

The language the writer uses is usually quite straightforward and easy to understand but he does also use some formal language like "monetary bribes" which suggest that he is writing for a broadsheet newspaper and an educated audience. However, some of his language is quite chatty and he uses slang like "clip you round the ear" which suggests that he's not always being serious.

IMPROVEMENTS NEEDED

▶ A better answer would be structured less around description/narrative and would concentrate more on analysis and explanation of the points made.

▶ The response should be more directly focused on how the writer views homework and how the references used show this.

▶ There needs to be more detailed explanation about how the examples of content which have been chosen indicate that the writer has some doubts about the value of homework. Remember: you have to convince the examiner that you have understood the question.

▶ More detailed explanation and comment about the writer's use of language would produce a better answer. There should be comment about some of the words the writer uses and why they help to create a particular response from the reader.

▶ Comments about language should be more precisely focused on specific examples rather than generalised assertions.

A better answer

This is a better answer, which includes many of these suggestions:

The writer clearly thinks that doing homework is a waste of time, especially when it seems to be common practice that it's done by parents instead of children. This point is conveyed by the catchy headline "Whose history essay is it anyway?" and the photograph with the article which shows a schoolboy looking fed up because his father is going through "one of his rebellious phases" and can't see the point of doing his Latin homework any more. The joke here is that the language of the boy's thoughts is like that which we usually associate with parents when they complain about their children's attitudes to school work.

In fact, the whole article is written in a rather humorous tone. The writer starts off by reversing the roles of parents and children and makes great use of applying vocabulary usually connected with children to the parents. For example, he talks about parents being "sensitive" and "under great emotional pressure". The whole situation seems to be one in which the children have the upper hand by "blackmailing" their parents into doing homework because they, the parents, don't want their children to be ridiculed in class because their efforts were not good enough.

However, the writer also makes the point that, much as parents want to help their children to do well, they also realise that as you grow older, many of the things which seemed to be so important when you were at school are of no use at all in real life. Studying Latin would seem to have been a particular waste of time if all it can do is enable you to talk to a table and there really is no point in committing factual details like the length of the Nile to memory when they can easily be looked up in a book. He then goes on to suggest ways that parents can avoid the chore of having to do homework, such as by using the internet or hiring intelligent au pairs. These seem to be somewhat extreme methods and the use of hyperbole helps to emphasise how pointless the whole thing is.

The writer does seem to have a more serious point under the generally light-hearted tone, however. He is certainly questioning the relevance of much of what is required to be learnt in schools and he does this by mentioning that great writers and thinkers such as Solomon, Shakespeare and Chaucer never did homework whereas minor modern celebrities did. This suggests that maybe homework is a waste of time, especially as those mentioned as having done it tend to be names of people we may not necessarily take seriously. Towards the end of the article, the writer adopts a more formal tone and makes his point through this mock seriousness. He uses words like "children might be genetically programmed to find homework irksome" and that they should be given the treatment of "monetary bribes". In the context of the article as a whole this overstatement produces an ironic effect. This is further emphasised by the deliberately colloquial closing statement which puts everything back into perspective and makes us realise that one of the main points the writer is making is how easy it is to cheat by getting someone else to do your coursework and homework and if such cheating takes place it really ought to be punished and not accepted as normal practice.

Typical exam question

The article *Bouncing back* gives advice on coping with bullying.

By close reference to the form, layout and language of the article:

1 **Explain the audience for whom the article has been written.**   [5 marks]

2 **Explore how successful you think the writer has been in appealing to that audience.**   [15 marks]

Stamp Out Bullying!

Bouncing

BULLYING: Mizz DIAGNOSIS

If anyone's ever told you bullying's just part of growing up, erase that from your memory now. Unlike periods and spots, being picked on isn't something you have to learn to deal with. And it's wrong to think you're weak if you can't cope. It's a major problem that leaves you feeling scared and lonely. In fact, it can totally wreck your confidence.

Some people get so depressed about being bullied that they need counselling. For others, suicide seems to be the only option. Just last September, 12-year-old Emma Morrison from Edinburgh decided to end her own life rather than face her bullies for one more day. It sounds drastic but, sadly, she's not the only one who's felt like there's no way out.

You can get through it, though. If you're being bullied, you have the power to turn the situation around and become a stronger person. Look at Victoria Beckham, Eminem and Gareth Gates. They were all bullied when they were younger, but now they're all mega-strong and an inspiration to loads of people. You can be, too. Just take a seat in our bully clinic and we'll try and patch you up. You'll be on the road to recovery in no time…

When you're down, there's only one thing to do: jump right up again…

back

WE PRESCRIBE: VACCINATION

Protect yourself against the bullying bug…

Whether you've got a problem with a bully or not, you can actively prevent a culture from developing by making your school a "no tolerance" zone. Your school should have its own anti-bullying policy anyway, but you can still help keep the corridors fear-free. Call a meeting with your teachers and organise a survey so everyone can have their say. Suggest having an anti-bullying week or create an anonymous comments box for people to pop their concerns into.

Loads of schools have peer-counselling schemes, too, where older pupils talk through problems with younger students. So set one up. If you raise awareness and get people talking, a potential bully will think twice about teasing someone.

WE PRESCRIBE: MEDICATION

Treat the symptoms of the bullying bug…

First off, don't spend your weekends trying to work out why you're being picked on. It's not your fault. Often, it's just bullies' way of making themselves feel better and more secure about their own lives. You'd be doing yourself down if you tried to change in any way, cos there's nothing wrong with you. We love you just the way you are. Tempting as it is to bunk off school so that you can avoid being bullied, your place is at your desk. Each time you shout, "Here" when your teacher takes the morning register, you triumph over your bullies. That way, you're showing them you've got a right to be there and they're not gonna win. Besides, you don't want to end up falling behind, do you? Whenever the bullies are on your back and you're feeling low, remind yourself of everything you've got going for you. C'mon, there's tons! Think of your friends and family that love you, your obsession for Justin T, the hobbies you're fab at. Write down all your talents, and any compliments people pay you. Now feel those positive thoughts flow through you. But if it's still getting you down, give ChildLine a call on 0800-1111 or email Help@bullyingonline.co.uk. There are people out there you can talk to and trust.

Annoyingly, bullies always seem to know exactly how to wind you up. But try not to show 'em that they're affecting you. They're looking for a reaction and will get a kick out of knowing you're upset or angry. No matter what they say to you, stay calm. The next time someone disses you, why not try saying (pleasantly and politely), "You're entitled to your opinion," and leave it at that? Don't get into a slanging match, though – it might escalate into something worse. Probably the best thing to do is ignore them. It's tough but they'll get bored eventually, honest!

When you're out and about, remember to stand tall. If you shuffle along with your head down, hoping not to get noticed, a bully might think you're an easy target. The more invisible you try to be, the more you tend to stick out. Instead, you wanna be striding when you walk, with your head held high. Practise it now in your mirror. Next time you go through the school gates, you'll send out the message that you're strong, confident and won't tolerate bullying. It works – even if you're shaking inside.

It's really helpful to learn some avoidance tactics. If you get bullied in the playground at lunchtimes, go and sit somewhere else. If it means hanging out in the canteen with loads of staff, then so be it. Yeah, it's unfair that you have to stay indoors, but while it's getting resolved, it'll help. Similarly, try to go to the loo in a group, and sit near the driver on the school bus. If you walk home, change your route whenever you can, so there's no chance the bully could be waiting for you somewhere.

In sticky situations, like if a gang confronts you, stay calm. Look 'em in the eye and ask them firmly to stop. Don't fight back. It solves nothing and might make things worse. If they're demanding cash, hand it over. Remember, you're more valuable than a pile of pennies. Then leave as soon as you can, and go spill to the nearest adult.

Bullying's a massive blow to your confidence. So how 'bout taking up self-defence, judo or karate? Not so you can bash 'em though. It'll help rebuild your courage cos you'll know you can defend yourself if you ever need to. Even if that's not your thing, you should still start a new hobby or join a youth club. You'll meet new friends and your self-esteem will soar.

WE PRESCRIBE: A CURE

Flush the bullying bug right out of your system…

The only way you're gonna rid yourself of the bullying bug is to tell someone what's going on. It can be any adult you trust – your ma, gran, dad, sis, anyone. If you need support, take a friend with you. If talking about it is too tough, write it down in a letter. Lots of people find it helps to keep a diary about what's been happening…

Alternatively, you can talk to a teacher. Your school has an obligation to protect you from bullies. But they need to know about it first. If you're not sure how to bring it up, pretend you need some homework help and stay behind after class so you can have a quiet word with your teacher. Or get your folks to go and see the Head. Don't worry, they won't tell everyone about it in assembly the next morning. If the bullying doesn't stop and you feel your school's not doing enough, your folks can make a formal complaint to the Local Education Authority. But if you're still not happy, you could always discuss moving schools. It might seem a bit extreme, but you don't have to stay put and suffer.

You're not being a grass when you tell an adult about a bully. You're just fighting for the right to live your life how you want. Feeling better yet?

AFTER-CARE

Oh, just one more thing. Even after the bullying stops, it'll still take you time to get over what's happened. So don't give yourself a hard time. You'll need time to recover.

What are the key words in this question?

- *Form* This refers to the type of article which it is; for example, is it a narrative story, a newspaper or magazine article, an interview, etc.?

- *Layout* This refers to the ways in which print, headlines, photographs, illustrations, etc. are included in the article.

- *Explain* State your understanding based on what you have interpreted from the **analysis** of layout, content and language.

- *Audience* This refers to the particular group of people to whom the article is intended to appeal.

- *Explore* Write at some length about the different ways in which the writer sets out to interest his or her chosen audience.

Lyndsay's Grade **A** answer

1. This article would seem to have been written for a teenage magazine. Its headline is colourful and informal in appearance and it uses different colours of print throughout the article. The article is broken up by sub-headings and at the end a final point is emphasised by being placed within a circle which makes it stand out from the rest of the article. The overall appearance of the page is friendly and informal and this would be likely to appeal to a teenage audience as they wouldn't feel threatened by something which looks too much like a text book. There is a photograph of people's faces and all of them are smiling; this would help to reassure readers who might be worried about being bullied themselves. All the faces in the photograph are of girls which would seem to suggest that this is a magazine aimed mainly at girls.

2. The article is also laid out to look like it's giving advice for dealing with an illness or medical problem as each section begins with the words "We prescribe" and contains illustrations of medicine being poured into a spoon. As well as this, each paragraph has a cross at the start. The cross is associated with first aid and this clever piece of layout also succeeds in making the readers realise that the issue they are dealing with is a serious one but one which can be cured.

The comparison with a medical article runs all the way through the article. The words "vaccination", "medication" and "a cure" are all highlighted in bold black type and they're all presented as part of the process of dealing with the bullying bug. A bug is usually thought of as something which is irritating and inconvenient but not particularly serious and so this again suggests that although bullying may be annoying, it can be cured if you follow the right procedure. The language used throughout the article is colloquial and friendly in tone, for example, it uses abbreviations like "cos". The writer also uses the second person pronoun "you" so the reader feels that she is being spoken to personally and is therefore more likely to take note of much of the good advice that it contains. The tone of the article seems to hit exactly the right note; the content indicates that the writer has a very thorough knowledge of the many different issues concerned with bullying, but does not present them in a dull or boring way and also does not talk down to the readers. It's friendly and comforting and shows concern and understanding – the closing question "Feeling better yet?" is very effective and overall the article is very successful in achieving its purpose.

What makes this a good answer?

► Lyndsay's comments are **clearly focused on the question**. The first sentence states who the audience for the article is and this is followed by explanations which are fully illustrated by **quotations and references**.

► The answer is a very full one; Lyndsay not only appreciates that this is a magazine article aimed at teenage girls but **explains her reasons** for concluding this.

► All the elements of the question are fully covered in both parts of the answer in such a way that a **full overall understanding** is revealed. A less good answer would simply make the points as a list without connecting them together.

► Lyndsay is not afraid to look for and explain some **more inferential details**, e.g. by linking the red crosses to the idea of first aid and healing.

► There is a **clearly stated conclusion** in which Lyndsay sums up the points made and brings her answer back to the question being answered.

Key skill: analysing the use of print and image

1

If a question asks you to write about the use of **print and image** (this may also be referred to as layout or presentation) you should think about:

- how the words look on the page (the font style and size; use of bold, italic or underlining and colour, shading, etc.);
- the use of headlines, captions, subheadings, bullet points;
- the use of illustrations, photographs, graphs, statistical tables, etc.;
- the way the material is presented on the page. For example, the relationship between text and image (are illustrations integral to the written text or are they placed apart from it? Is the page set out as landscape or portrait? Are borders or other design features used?).

2

To gain a Grade C and above, it is important that you explain how these various features are used to create a particular effect. Simply describing them is unlikely to give evidence that you have understood how they have been used.

3

A good answer will make good use of **appropriate terminology** such as that used in the bullet points above. You should become familiar with these terms but keep in mind that this is an English exam and not a Media Studies one. You will not be required to use the specialist jargon you may have learnt when studying that subject!

DON'T FORGET ...

✓ When writing about media texts you must show that you understand the writer's **purpose and attitude** and how these are communicated to the reader.

✓ You will be expected to explain how print and image are used as well as language and how they have an effect on the reader.

✓ You should be prepared to **give your own personal response** and explain how the article affects you and why it does so.

✓ At all times you should **justify any comment** you make by using evidence – references to or quotations from the text.

✓ You must express yourself precisely and **your arguments should be clearly structured**; the easier you make it for the examiner to follow what you are saying, the better the mark you are likely to gain.

✓ You should show awareness of **the writer's use of fact and opinion**. Media texts are often intended to **persuade** you to agree with a point of view and you should comment on how the writer sets out to achieve this. You should consider the effects achieved by the use of **emotive language** (words and phrases that appeal to the emotions rather than the head).

What the examiners are looking for

To achieve a Grade C when writing about media texts you should:

1 Make a clear, competent attempt to engage with media concepts.

This means that you should give a clear indication that you understand the purpose for which the text was produced.

2 Write a structured response which selects and comments on different aspects of the text.

As always, you should keep a clear focus on the question; you may have to write about different media features (layout, the use of images, etc.) so you should make sure that you quote or refer to appropriate examples.

3 Make competent use of some appropriate technical terminology.

You should be able to use correctly terms such as *headline*, *caption*, etc.

4 Show a clear appreciation of the links between image and text and give a clear explanation of how layout and presentation contribute to the writer's effects.

You should be able to make relevant comments about how photographs, illustrations and other such devices are used to influence the audience.

To achieve a Grade A when writing about media texts you should:

1 Show a clear and detailed understanding and explanation of how form, layout and presentation are used.

You should show a complete understanding of how the different media features used in the text combine to create the intended effect on the target audience.

2 Construct careful and logically structured arguments and explanations.

Your answer should deal fully with all aspects of the task and develop logically towards a conclusion which provides an answer to the question and shows that you have a complete understanding of what is required by it.

3 Make sure that references to and quotations/examples from the text are fully absorbed into the answer and shaped for purpose.

The comments you make should be explained in detail and supported by appropriate quotations and references which are fully focused on the question.

4 Show a sophisticated and convincing use of technical terminology to describe media features.

You should be confident in your use of media terminology in support of your comments. This means that you should use it naturally as and when appropriate but not just to show off that you know the terms!

Typical exam question

Compare Passage 1, a non-fiction text, with the two media texts, Passages 2a and 2b.

Compare:
- **the form, layout and presentation of the articles**
- **what they have to say**
- **the language used to say it.**   [20 marks]

Passage 1

The walls of Marrakesh reflect this red land with a beguiling rosy glow which deepens as the afternoon light fades. Running unbroken for over 6 miles, their towers and battlements throw a spectacular cloak around the city. But if Fez was enclosed, almost hidden away behind its walls, Marrakesh is bursting out of them. The new town pushes right up close. It's colourful and expansive with broad avenues and a Las Vegas-like dazzle and swagger. Slab-like resort hotels with names like Sahara Inn jostle alongside a brand new opera house. This is an old city desperate to accommodate the modern world.

I'm disappointed. I'd expected something exotic and unpredictable. After all, Marrakesh has the most romantic connotations of any city in this romantic country. Perhaps it's because the snow-capped range of mountains that frames the city in every tourist brochure is virtually invisible in the haze. Perhaps it's because almost everyone I've seen so far is white and European like me, or perhaps it's because I feel, on these tidy tree-lined streets that I could be anywhere.

Then someone suggests the Djemaa el-Fna.

To get to it I have to leave the wide streets and bland resort hotels of the New Town and pass inside the peach-red city walls through the twin arched gates of Bab er Rob and Bab Agnaou.

Once inside the gates the atmosphere is transformed. Tourist buses prowl, but they have to move at the pace of a largely African throng. The tallest building is not an international hotel but the elegant and decorative minaret of the Koutoubia mosque, rising to a majestic height of 230 feet, from which it has witnessed goings-on in the Djemaa el-Fna for over 800 years. There is an entirely unsubstantiated story that because the minaret directly overlooked a harem, only blind muezzins were allowed up it.

The Djemaa el-Fna is not a beautiful space. It's a distended rectangle, surrounded by an undistinguished clutter of buildings and lines of parked taxis. Its name translates as 'Assembly of the Dead', which is believed to refer to the practice of executing criminals here.

It's bewildering. There's so much noise that they could still be executing criminals, for all I know. There seems no focal point to the commotion – no psychic centre. At one end, where gates lead into the souk, tourists take tea on the café balconies and overlook the action from a safe distance. The locals favour the food stalls, which are drawn up in a circle at the centre of the Djemaa, like Western wagons waiting for an Indian attack. They are well-lit and the people serving the food have clean white coats and matching hats. This concession to First-World hygiene is deceptive. The rest of the Djemaa el-Fna is a realm way beyond protective clothing.

Sahara by Michael Palin

Passage 2a

Marrakech

Against the back-drop of the snow-capped peaks of the High Atlas and set in a 1000 year-old palm grove lies the Imperial City of Marrakech. Every morning as the sun rises over the ramparts, the population awakens to the call of the muezzin from the towering Koutoubia Mosque, and a multicoloured crowd flows into the medina. Another day has begun. Plunge yourself into the souk's fascinating maze of stalls and discover carpets in colourful designs, fine jewellery, hand-made pottery and numerous items crafted from wood, leather and wrought iron, as well as sweet

or pungent-smelling spices, oils and herbs. The focal point of Marrakech is the great Djemaa el-Fna square.

Providing an ever-changing source of entertainment, it undergoes an astonishing and magical transformation at dusk. Tourists and locals wander amongst the singers and dancers, snake charmers and story tellers. There are acrobats, tumblers and preachers, jugglers, magicians and rows of stalls selling a variety of mouth-watering foods including fresh citrus fruit. At one end you can take time to sit on a balcony and watch the whole spectacle as you sip a glass of mint tea. It is often called 'the greatest free show on earth' – though you are expected to pay for taking pictures or filming. Marrakech is rich in restaurants serving delicious local cuisine in atmospheric settings but even more exotic is a visit to a Fantasia – a lavish Berber dinner where, after a wholesome feast, the amazing cabaret is performed in a great open arena.

Cadogan Holiday Morocco Brochure, 2002–2003

Passage 2b

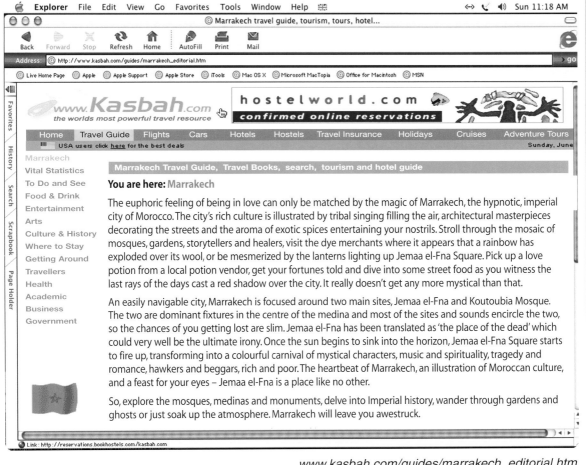

Explorer   File   Edit   View   Go   Favorites   Tools   Window   Help   ⊞   ⟷ ℂ 𝅘 Sun 11:18 AM

@ Marrakech travel guide, tourism, tours, hotel...

Back   Forward   Stop   Refresh   Home   AutoFill   Print   Mail   e

Address: @ http://www.kasbah.com/guides/marrakech_editorial.htm   › go

@ Live Home Page   @ Apple   @ Apple Support   @ Apple Store   @ iTools   @ Mac OS X   @ Microsoft MacTopia   @ Office for Macintosh   @ MSN

www.**Kasbah**.com
the worlds most powerful travel resource

hostelworld.com
confirmed online reservations

Home | Travel Guide | Flights | Cars | Hotels | Hostels | Travel Insurance | Holidays | Cruises | Adventure Tours

🇺🇸 USA users click here for the best deals   Sunday, June

Marrakech Travel Guide, Travel Books, search, tourism and hotel guide

Marrakech
Vital Statistics
To Do and See
Food & Drink
Entertainment
Arts
Culture & History
Where to Stay
Getting Around
Travellers
Health
Academic
Business
Government

You are here: Marrakech

The euphoric feeling of being in love can only be matched by the magic of Marrakech, the hypnotic, imperial city of Morocco. The city's rich culture is illustrated by tribal singing filling the air, architectural masterpieces decorating the streets and the aroma of exotic spices entertaining your nostrils. Stroll through the mosaic of mosques, gardens, storytellers and healers, visit the dye merchants where it appears that a rainbow has exploded over its wool, or be mesmerized by the lanterns lighting up Jemaa el-Fna Square. Pick up a love potion from a local potion vendor, get your fortunes told and dive into some street food as you witness the last rays of the days cast a red shadow over the city. It really doesn't get any more mystical than that.

An easily navigable city, Marrakech is focused around two main sites, Jemaa el-Fna and Koutoubia Mosque. The two are dominant fixtures in the centre of the medina and most of the sites and sounds encircle the two, so the chances of you getting lost are slim. Jemaa el-Fna has been translated as 'the place of the dead' which could very well be the ultimate irony. Once the sun begins to sink into the horizon, Jemaa el-Fna Square starts to fire up, transforming into a colourful carnival of mystical characters, music and spirituality, tragedy and romance, hawkers and beggars, rich and poor. The heartbeat of Marrakech, an illustration of Moroccan culture, and a feast for your eyes – Jemaa el-Fna is a place like no other.

So, explore the mosques, medinas and monuments, delve into Imperial history, wander through gardens and ghosts or just soak up the atmosphere. Marrakech will leave you awestruck.

Link: http://reservations.bookhostels.com/kasbah.com

www.kasbah.com/guides/marrakech_editorial.htm

What are the key words in this question?

- *Compare*   This means that you should write in some detail about not just the similarities in the passages, but also the **differences**.

- *Non-fiction text*   This is a piece of writing whose main purpose is to **provide information in a factual way**.

- *Media text*   This is a piece of writing whose main purpose is to **persuade or influence** the reader into sharing the writer's point of view. It is likely to use pictures, illustrations and other presentational devices as well as print.

- *Form*   The form of an article could be that of a newspaper article, an advertisement, a website, an extract from an autobiography, etc.

- *Layout and presentation*   These words refer to the ways the material is set out on the page and its overall appearance; they are very important issues to consider when analysing the effect of a media text.

- *What they have to say*   This means you should write about the content of the articles.

- *Language*   This refers to the words used by the writers, the **tone of voice** they use, the range and **variety of sentence structures**, and the effects they achieve through the use of similes, metaphors and other **figures of speech**.

Sarah's Grade **C** answer

Michael Palin's description of Marrakesh is set out in paragraphs and looks as if it has been taken from a book. The second passage is from a holiday brochure and contains some photographs of the country. These make this passage seem more eye-catching. The third passage is from a website.

All three passages are about Marrakesh in Morocco. At first, Michael Palin isn't very impressed; he thinks the place is colourful but he's disappointed because it isn't very romantic and that it's just like anywhere else. He uses words like "slab-like" and "bland" to describe the hotels. However, when he visits the Djemaa el-Fna he finds somewhere which is different; it's not a beautiful space but it's full of local people (the rest of the town seemed to be full of white European tourists) and is much more bewildering because of the noise. His attitude towards it seems to be a little uncertain; he says it's "undistinguished" and it sounds as if criminals are being executed there. His last sentence suggests that it's also not very hygienic.

The writer in Passage 1 is describing somewhere that he's visited and is trying to

GOOD POINTS

This is a potentially good answer but doesn't make the most of the points it mentions.

CONSISTENTLY COMPARATIVE APPROACH: Sarah makes a good attempt throughout her answer to compare the different passages and shows that she has a good understanding of the differences in their content.

USE OF QUOTATIONS: Sarah's answer also shows a good understanding of the difference in the tone and purpose of the passages and uses relevant quotations to support this. She also makes some attempt to explain how these quotations help to convey the writers' points of view.

FOCUS ON TASK: Sarah keeps the requirements of the task clearly in mind; her introductory paragraph states her intention clearly and her conclusion returns to the main point of the task.

help the readers understand what he thinks about the place. The writers of the other two passages are trying to persuade their readers to come and visit Marrakesh and so they write about the town in a much more attractive way. Both of them talk about how attractive the sunset is there and use words like "magic", "hypnotic" and "mesmerised" to suggest that it's very exotic. The writers of these passages also talk directly to the reader, e.g. "Plunge yourself", whereas Michael Palin just describes things from his point of view.

IMPROVEMENTS NEEDED

▶ Sarah needs to adopt a more **consistently analytical approach**. Remember that in this type of question, the examiner wants you to show *how* a writer achieves a particular effect. Sarah tends to describe the similarities and differences between the passages without making any detailed comments on them. This is particularly the case with the comments on the layout and presentation of the passages where the only comment is that the use of pictures makes the brochure more 'eye-catching'. A better answer would have developed this comment.

▶ More detailed references would lead to evidence of clearer understanding.

▶ Greater **depth and detail** in the comments would show a more thorough understanding of what the writers are trying to do. For example, Sarah's comments on Michael Palin's attitudes are insufficiently developed to show whether or not she has understood them fully.

▶ It's a good approach to think to yourself 'Why?' after every statement you make and then answer that question in the next sentence you write.

Niral's Grade **A** answer

An answer which followed this advice would read something like this:

All three passages write about the Moroccan city of Marrakesh. Passage 1, by Michael Palin, is an extract from a piece of travel writing, and records the writer's impressions of the city; his concern is to record these honestly and to give a clear account to the reader of what the town seemed like to him. The other two passages are written with a different purpose as they are from a travel brochure and a website, both of which are trying to attract their readers to visit the city. Consequently, the language they use is more emotive and they also make use of photographs which illustrate the exotic beauty and appeal of the town and which are intended to attract and interest the reader. The extract from the holiday brochure also uses different colours of print which makes it look far more interesting than the formal layout of Palin's travel book.

Michael Palin begins by describing the new town of Marrakesh; he finds it rather disappointing as it appears to have deliberately set out to lose its traditional qualities and attract tourists by building hotel blocks which are exactly the same as those to be found anywhere else in the world. He describes them as "bland" and "slab-like" with a "Las Vegas-like dazzle and swagger" which suggests that he considers them to be rather garish and unattractive. Marrakesh is "an old city desperate to accommodate the modern world". The word "desperate" shows that he thinks that Marrakesh is not being particularly successful.

However, when he visits the Djemaa el-Fna, he finds it much more interesting. The single sentence paragraph "Then someone suggests the Djemaa el-Fna" is a very effective way of emphasising the importance of this visit. It is when he starts to describe this place that the most direct comparisons can be made with the other articles. They both emphasise that this is the part of Marrakesh which tourists are likely to find most attractive. They do this by using language which emphasises it as being a place which is beyond the everyday experience of most people by using vocabulary which presents us with positive images of the place. We are told about the exciting entertainment to be found there consisting of, for example, acrobats and magicians; the food on sale is "mouth-watering" and "delicious"; "the magic of Marrakesh" is compared to "the euphoric feeling of being in love". Wherever you go you are surrounded by "the aroma of exotic spices"; you can "pick up a love potion from a local potion vendor" and watch the "mystical beauty" of the sunset. The square is a "carnival of mystical characters" and is full of life - a far cry from its name which means "the place of the dead".

All of these descriptions and activities are intended to attract the readers to visit a place which is presented to them as exotic and mystical; the writers of the passages are concerned with this alone. Michael Palin mentions many of the same things; for example, he mentions the square's name as meaning the place of the dead, but gives it a more sinister interpretation by saying that the name derives from the practice of executing criminals there; he then suggests that these executions might still be going on with the amount of noise which can be heard. Because he is not trying to encourage people to visit, his impressions are quite honest. He finds the atmosphere "bewildering" with "no focal point" and "no psychic centre". He is more cautious when writing about the food; although he mentions the appearance of hygiene, his final paragraph is more critical and this reflects the tone of his whole description. The other passages conclude with more positive statements referring to "amazing cabarets" and Marrakesh leaving you awestruck which reflects the different purpose of their writers.

What makes this a good answer?

► Niral has shown a **good overall understanding** of all three passages.

► He has made a consistent attempt to compare the passages following the guidance of the question.

► This overall understanding is reinforced by Niral's references to **specific details**.

► The response covers all elements of the question but, in particular, Niral shows a good appreciation of the writers' use of language and how it is tailored to a specific audience and for different purposes.

► His comments are backed up by **quotations and references** and, in turn, these are explained to the reader.

► Niral's concluding sentence **focuses directly on the question** and provides a direct answer to it.

Key skill: making cross-references

1

Show a clear awareness of the **purpose and audience** of each text. This will give you and the examiner a clear point of reference for the comments you are going to make.

3

Try to adopt a **consistently analytical approach**. Don't write about each text independently and then try to make points of comparison in a concluding paragraph.

2

It is best to start from an **overall standpoint**. For example, you could talk about the use of photographs and illustrations and then compare how the different texts make use of them.

4

You may find that it helps you to make a comparison by thinking which text you personally prefer and why, but you should try to relate this to how successful each has been in carrying out its specific purpose.

DON'T FORGET ...

✓ Writing a comparison means that you should show an understanding of what the passages have in common and also the differences between them.

✓ When you are comparing a non-fiction text with a media text you should show an awareness of the **different purposes and audiences** for which they were written and how they set out to appeal to them.

✓ You should always back up your comments with **quotations** from the passages or **references** to particular details of the content or of the layout/presentation.

✓ You do not have to say which of the passages you prefer unless the question particularly asks you to do so.

✓ It is not enough just to state differences and similarities; you must **explain** the effects the writers are trying to achieve by **commenting on the techniques** they use.

✓ It is the ability to respond perceptively to the ways the writers use language which is likely to identify the best answers. In particular, consider the devices such as humour, emotive language, etc. which are used by the writers, and how effective their use is.

✓ Don't be afraid to refer to your own **personal response** to the passages; if they have a particular effect on you (for example, if you feel that you have been persuaded to share the writer's point of view), explain what has done this – what works with you is likely to work with other readers.

✓ Look closely at the ways the writers use **fact and opinion** and, particularly with the media texts, whether opinions have been presented as if they are facts (a fact is something which can be proved by external evidence; an opinion is simply what the writer thinks is so).

What the examiners are looking for

To achieve a Grade C when comparing non-fiction and media texts you should:

1 Write a structured and full response.

You must organise your answer so that the line of your argument is clear and covers all aspects of the task.

2 Show a clear attempt to engage with media concepts.

You should make it clear that you have a sound understanding of the purpose of a media text and what distinguishes it from other types of writing. To do this you should show that you are familiar with appropriate terminology.

3 Explain clearly how form, layout, presentation and content contribute to the effect of the text.

The important point here is that you make a consistent attempt to explain how these features contribute to the overall effect of the text.

4 Show some appreciation of the way the writers use language.

Explain how the writer's choice of words helps you to understand meanings and inferences.

Support this understanding with appropriate quotation and reference.

To achieve a Grade A when comparing non-fiction and media texts you should:

1 Write a complete answer, covering all elements of the question and adopting a consistently comparative approach.

You must show an appreciation of the whole task and compare the texts by relating specific details to an overview, explaining and justifying your points and references.

2 Show a full understanding of what the task requires.

You should structure your answer so that it is fully focused on the question and include clear reasons for and evaluations of your comments.

3 Show a clear and detailed understanding of how form, content, layout, presentation and language contribute to the effect of a text.

You must refer to all the elements of the question and show a consistently analytical approach to explaining how the writers make use of them. Don't be afraid to include your personal responses as long as you can justify them by reference to the texts. At this level, well-developed and fully justified explanations of the writers' use of language to achieve their purpose are particularly important.

4 Show careful and logical organisation.

Material should be fully absorbed and shaped for the purpose with a consistently comparative approach and a conclusion which clearly attempts to answer the question.

5 Show a sophisticated and convincing use of critical terminology to describe media concepts.

You should be fully confident in your use of technical terms as part of your overall response; A Grade responses are distinguished by the fact that these terms are absorbed into the answer and indicate that the writer is thoroughly familiar with them without feeling the need to explain them every time they are used.

I POETRY FROM DIFFERENT CULTURES

Typical exam question

Compare *Island Man* with *Blessing* showing how poets convey their feelings about the particular cultures they are writing about.   [20 marks]

Island Man

(For a Caribbean island man in London who still wakes up to the sound of the sea.)

Morning
and island man wakes up
to the sound of blue surf
in his head
the steady breaking and wombing

wild seabirds
and fishermen pushing out to sea
the sun surfacing defiantly
from the east
of his small emerald island
he always comes back   groggily groggily

Comes back to sands
of a grey metallic soar   to surge of wheels
to dull North Circular roar

muffling muffling
his crumpled pillow waves
island man heaves himself

Another London day

                                        Grace Nichols

Blessing

The skin cracks like a pod.
There never is enough water.

Imagine the drip of it,
the small splash, echo
in a tin mug,
the voice of a kindly god.
Sometimes, the sudden rush
of fortune. The municipal pipe bursts,
silver crashes to the ground
and the flow has found
a roar of tongues. From the huts,
a congregation: every man woman
child for streets around
butts in, with pots,
brass, copper, aluminium,
plastic buckets,
frantic hands,

and naked children
screaming in the liquid sun,
their highlights polished to perfection,
flashing light,
as the blessing sings
over their small bones.

Imtiaz Dharker

What are the key words in this question?

● **Compare**   This means you should write about both **similarities and differences** between the poems. You can compare them in different ways such as content, style and language, etc.

● **Convey**   This means that you have to show an understanding of the ways in which the poets communicate their **thoughts and feelings** to the reader. You must show that you understand what the poems are saying and how the way in which they're written relates to this. You should write about the **structure and form** of the poems and, in particular, about the poets' **use of language** (imagery, metaphors, similes, choice of vocabulary, etc.). Remember that **explaining** *how* these devices help your understanding is a key skill.

● **Cultures**   It is expected that your writing about poems will be informed by an appreciation of the **social, cultural and historical background** in which they were written. However, don't forget that this is an English and not a Sociology, Geography or History exam. Sometimes – especially when you're in an exam – it's very easy to fall back on repeating notes you may have made about the poets' backgrounds and lose sight of the fact that you should be writing about the poems themselves!

Neil's Grade C answer

Both of these poems are from different cultures. Grace Nichols is a Caribbean poet who lives in England and Imtiaz Dharker lives in India. They are both women. "Island Man" is set in England and describes how a Caribbean immigrant to this country still misses his homeland, especially the sea. In London, instead of waking up to the sound of the waves, all he can hear is the constant traffic on the North Circular Road near his house. The sounds of the sea and the sea birds are always in his head and even the "muffling" pillow on which he has been sleeping appears to have wave patterns. The last line of the poem "Another London day" is set out as a line on its own and seems to suggest how boring and uninteresting his life is now compared to what it was like in the Caribbean.

Grace Nichols is sympathetic to the feelings of the man she's describing as he's living in a foreign land but can't escape from the memories of the country where he was born where the weather was much warmer and the life was more relaxed. In the Caribbean there is sun and "blue surf" but London is "dull" and "grey".

In "Blessing" Imtiaz Dharker writes about how important water is to some people in different parts of the world especially in somewhere like India. "There never is enough

GOOD POINTS

UNDERSTANDING OF THE TEXT: Neil has shown a **clear understanding** of what both poems are about and paraphrased their ideas quite thoroughly. He has included some **quotations**, especially from *Island Man*, and has made an attempt to explain how they help to convey the poet's thoughts.

FOCUS ON THE QUESTION: The opening paragraph indicates that there is a clear awareness of the need to compare the two poems and makes a sound attempt to do this. Neil's comments on both poems also indicate that he understands the need to explain the ways the poets write about their cultures.

water" she says. She asks you to imagine the sound as it drips into a tin mug and says that it is like the voice of a kindly god. Sometimes the town water pipe bursts and the people are able to have a bonus supply of water so they rush out to collect as much as they can in all sorts of containers from brass pots to plastic buckets. The young children of the town dance naked in the water which the poet describes as a blessing.

Imtiaz Dharker tells us how much water is depended on by people of different cultures. It is seen as something holy and precious as it is described as a being like a god and a blessing. The poem makes us realise that something we may take for granted is really very important to people's lives.

IMPROVEMENTS NEEDED

► SUMMARY OR ANALYSIS? Although Neil's answer indicates that he has a good understanding of the poems, this is mainly through explaining what they are about in his own words. In fact, the comments on *Blessing* read very much as if they are remembered class notes and would benefit from being more closely rooted in the text.

► REFERENCE TO THE TEXT: Neil's textual references are somewhat superficial and could be improved by more detailed comment; what effect do the poets achieve by their choice of vocabulary, the use of repetition, etc.?

► FOCUS ON THE QUESTION: Neil's answer could also be improved by making more consistent and specific comparisons between the poems.

Michelle's Grade A answer

This answer includes many of the suggestions made on the previous page:

Both "Island Man" and "Blessing" begin by referring to water. In "Island Man" it is the sound of the "blue surf" with its "steady breaking and wombing" which is in the head of the Caribbean man waking up in the midst of London's "dull North Circular roar". The poet, Grace Nichols, presents us with the experience of this man living in a culture different from that of where he was born. There, the morning suggests life and vitality; the sun surfaces "defiantly" and the fishermen are "pushing out to sea" to the sound of the "wild seabirds" from his "small emerald island". Words such as "defiantly" and "steady" suggest strength and purpose and the reference to "emerald" gives the impression that there is a precious permanence about his island home. The "wild seabirds" give us the idea of freedom and the difficult word "wombing" describing the sea suggests that the sea, such an important feature of the man's life, is responsible for giving birth to all life on earth.

Ironically, "Island Man" has left his Caribbean home to live in a much larger island where he is not in close proximity to the freedom and life of the sea which is so much part of the culture in which he was born. He wakes up slowly and with difficulty; this is emphasised by the repetition of "groggily groggily" as the sounds of his dream blend into the sound of the traffic outside his room. The poet cleverly transposes vocabulary here, as "soar" and "surge" are words more commonly associated with the sea. Finally he wakes, leaving his dreams on his pillow, to the monotony of "Another London day". Grace Nichols has effectively conveyed to the reader how powerfully someone's background influences their life and no matter where they are, how difficult it is to escape from the culture you were born into.

To Imtiaz Dharker, water is seen as something which is essential to life and how, in her culture, it is a precious blessing. The parched land "cracks like a pod" as water is scarce. Simply to imagine the sound of it – the poet refers to a "drip" which to us would seem a very insignificant amount – is like hearing "the voice of a kindly god". This makes us understand how much water is seen as a blessing. The rest of the poem describes a particular incident when the municipal water pipe burst. This occurrence is seen as something of a mixed blessing. The people of the town rush out to collect water as the drip has now turned into "a roar of tongues" calling them. They use whatever containers they can find to preserve this blessed substance, collecting it with "frantic hands". Presumably, the townspeople are aware that the burst pipe could mean problems with the water supply in the coming days. The innocent, naked children, however, look upon the gushing water as a "liquid sun" and perform a dance of joy as it "sings over their small bones". The last line reminds us of the joy and comfort which water brings but also of its importance in ensuring that "small bones" are able to grow and develop. By presenting us with a vivid snapshot of this incident, the poet conveys how essential water is to her culture and how precious such a blessing is.

II POETRY FROM THE ENGLISH LITERARY HERITAGE

Typical exam question

Compare *The Lake Isle of Innisfree* with *Upon Westminster Bridge* and show how the poets have used language and imagery to convey a sense of peace and tranquillity.   [20 marks]

The Lake Isle of Innisfree

I will arise and go now, and go to Innisfree,
And a small cabin build there, of clay and wattles made:
Nine bean-rows will I have there, a hive for the honey-bee,
And live alone in the bee-loud glade.

And I shall have some peace there, for peace comes dropping slow,
Dropping from the veils of the morning to where the cricket sings;
There midnight's all a glimmer, and noon a purple glow,
And evening full of the linnet's wings.

I will arise and go now, for always night and day
I hear lake water lapping with low sounds by the shore;
While I stand on the roadway, or on the pavements grey,
I hear it in the deep heart's core.

William Butler Yeats (1865–1939)

Upon Westminster Bridge

Earth has not anything to show more fair:
Dull would he be of soul who could pass by
A sight so touching in its majesty:
This city now doth, like a garment, wear
The beauty of the morning; silent, bare,
Ships, towers, domes, theatres and temples lie
Open unto the fields, and to the sky;
All bright and glittering in the smokeless air.
Never did sun more beautifully steep
In his first splendour, valley, rock, or hill;
Ne'er saw I, never felt, a calm so deep!
The river glideth at his own sweet will:
Dear God! the very houses seem asleep;
And all that mighty heart is lying still!

William Wordsworth (1770–1850)
(Composed upon Westminster Bridge, 3rd September 1802)

What are the key words in this question?

● *Language and imagery*   These words are telling you that your response should include an understanding of the effects achieved by the words the poets use. Imagery refers particularly to the **similes and metaphors** contained in the poems; language covers such things as the use of rhyme, rhythm and other poetic devices as well as the poet's choice of vocabulary. Remember that simply identifying poetic devices is not enough: you must explain their effect.

● *Peace and tranquillity*   Again, these are words which should help you to **focus your response**; they tell you that the poems are intended to create such feelings and you should use this knowledge to structure your answer.

Lorna's Grade **A** answer

Both Yeats and Wordsworth write about peace and tranquillity. Yeats is in the middle of a city, surrounded by "pavements grey" (the unusual word order places particular emphasis on the dull colour) and is dreaming of escaping to a secluded island which he knows in the middle of a lake in the Irish countryside. Wordsworth, writing at the time of the Industrial Revolution, is in the middle of London early in the morning and is surprised by the peace, quiet and beauty of the scene before him.

Yeats' poem begins with a statement implying decisive action: "I will arise and go now". He intends to leave his present surroundings and escape to the isle of Innisfree – no doubt the word's third syllable "free" reinforces its attraction. Once there, he wishes to live a simple, self-sufficient life; he'll build a simple cabin (nothing as grand as a house) made of natural materials ("clay and wattles"). He intends to plant "nine bean rows" and have a "hive for the honey bee". The precise number "nine" suggests the modesty of his ambition, but there may also be a suggestion that it possesses some mystical power as nine is a potent magic number and Yeats' poetry contains many references to Irish myths and legends. The next line also makes his intentions clear: he wishes to "live alone in the bee-loud glade" and the peaceful sounds are echoed in the onomatopoeia of the open vowel sounds in this line.

Life on the lake island will provide the poet with the peace that he wants. Indeed, peace seems to fill the whole surroundings as it comes "dropping slow" throughout the day. The repetition of the participle "dropping" effectively slows up the line to emphasise the peace he feels and which lasts all day "from the veils of the morning to where the cricket sings".

The final stanza of the poem takes us back to where it begins; the tranquillity of the lake island is at present only in the poet's imagination. Although in his mind he always hears the lake waters lapping, he is still standing in the roadways among the pavements grey (the harshness of the surroundings is emphasised by the harsher rhythm) and the poet realises his need to return to the place which is firmly fixed in his "deep heart's core".

The situation is somewhat reversed in the sonnet "Upon Westminster Bridge". Wordsworth is a poet usually associated with writing about the beauties of the countryside but in this poem he expresses pleasurable surprise at the beauty which can be found in a large city. London at this time in the morning is a sight "touching in its majesty". He has caught the city before it is awake and he is aware of the beauty of the buildings rather than the noise and bustle which is usually associated with them. Everything is "bright and glittering in the smokeless air". To the poet, this scene is more beautiful than anything he has ever witnessed in the countryside and he has never felt "a calm so deep". It is as if he has caught the city unawares and has been made aware of a glory within it as it sleeps with its mighty heart lying still. The final line of the poem reminds us of the tremendous power and strength in the industrial and commercial qualities of the city which are the attributes people usually associate with it.

In conclusion, both poets describe scenes of tranquillity, although Wordsworth is physically present in his whereas Yeats views his scene only in his mind. The language of both poems emphasises the beauties and special qualities of the places and both poets write in a measured, gentle rhythm which supports the scenes they are describing.

What makes this a good answer?

► **COMPARISON:** Lorna has shown a good understanding of the way the poets treat the same topic and has referred to this consistently throughout her answer. She has also clearly identified the **differences** in their situations and the way they have treated the subject.

► **ANALYTICAL APPROACH:** Particularly in her comments on *The Lake Isle of Innisfree*, Lorna has shown that she is aware of the complexities of the poet's thoughts and of the **meanings below the surface of the poem**.

► **LANGUAGE:** Lorna has shown a perceptive appreciation of the poets' **linguistic techniques** and has not only quoted relevantly in support of her comments, but has also explained how these quotations illustrate the point she is making.

► **TECHNICAL VOCABULARY:** Technical terms like *onomatopoeia* have been used correctly and with confidence but not self-consciously.

Key skill: comparison

1

All GCSE poetry tasks are likely to require you to compare at least two poems.

2

Remember that comparison means writing about **similarities** *and* **differences**.

3

Don't over-complicate your response. It is almost certain that the poems you are set to write about will be on a similar theme or topic which will provide you with an overall area for comparison. Once you have identified this then you should consider the different ways in which the different poems treat this topic. You can do this either by writing about the poems in turn and drawing points together in your conclusion, or by writing about them both together.

4

There are more things to compare than just topics and subject matter, for example, the form of the poems, the use of rhyme and rhythm, etc.

5

When you are revising and preparing for the exam it's a good idea to try to find how many different ways you can group poems together as well as by subject matter, e.g. by form (sonnets, odes, etc.); by date of composition; by background culture; poems written by women poets; poems which rhyme and poems which don't, and so on. How many other ways can you think of?

DON'T FORGET ...

✓ Writing about poetry requires you to look closely at the poet's **use of language** and, in particular, to be aware of the **associations** of the words used. There are no right or wrong interpretations of a poem and it is your job to identify the **different layers of meaning** which may be suggested by the poet's choice of words.

✓ **Precise and relevant quotation** from the poems is necessary to make your arguments convincing. However, you must make sure that you **justify** your reason for choosing a particular quotation and explain how it **illustrates the point** you are making.

✓ It is more effective to work short quotations from the poems into the fabric of your essay rather than quoting at length; remember to indicate quotations by placing them within inverted commas.

✓ When writing about poetry, you will need to refer to some **technical details** such as the poet's use of rhyme and rhythm and the regularity (or otherwise) of the poem's stanza pattern. Remember it is not enough simply to identify a rhyme scheme (abba abba, etc.); what matters is that you can **comment on the effects** the poet achieves by it.

✓ You will also be expected to have some knowledge of **technical vocabulary** (such as metaphor, alliteration, etc.). However, writing about poetry involves more than the ability to spot such literary devices ('There is some alliteration in this line…'); you must comment on **the effect achieved** (e.g. 'The use of alliteration effectively slows down the line…').

✓ You must express yourself clearly and coherently; think about what you are going to say before you start to write. **Focus your comments** clearly on the question and make sure that you conclude with a definite statement which refers back to it.

What the examiners are looking for

To achieve a Grade **C** your response to reading poetry must:

1 Show an effective use of quotation and reference to support your comments.

You must use quotations to show your understanding of what the poet is saying but you should also be able to explain how the quotations illustrate this.

2 Make some cross-references between different poems.

You should be able to write sensibly about the way different poets treat the same topics.

3 Show an awareness of the poet's techniques and purpose.

You should be able to indicate that you have some understanding of the ways in which the poets achieve their effects through their use of poetic devices.

4 Show an understanding of the poets' feelings, attitudes and ideas.

You must not only explain the surface meaning of the poems but show some awareness of the meaning beyond the literal.

To achieve a Grade **A** your response to reading poetry must:

1 Contain well-selected quotations and references closely integrated into your argument.

Your response must be tightly structured and the quotations you use should clearly and seamlessly be linked into your explanation of how the poets achieve their intentions.

2 Show close and detailed analysis of the poets' techniques.

You must be able to show a sensitive and consistently detailed appreciation of the poet's language, form and structure.

3 Show a sustained exploration of and sympathetic understanding of the poet's ideas and attitudes.

You must show a developed understanding both of the main points of the poem and also consistent and imaginative insight into the underlying issues and themes which the poet is expressing implicitly through the associations of language, imagery, etc.

4 Show a consistent and detailed appreciation of the relationships between two or more poems.

Your answer must show a consistently comparative approach; this does not mean that you have to write about both poems at the same time, but you must show a developed awareness of the different ways in which poets treat similar issues and themes.

Typical exam question

Write a letter to a cousin who is just about to start Year 7 at your school.

Describe some of the problems which might arise in the first week and explain how best to deal with them. Your letter should be lively and interesting and written from the point of view of someone who knows the ropes!

You do not need to include your address or the date. Begin your letter 'Dear...'

[20 marks]

What are the key words in this question?

- *Describe* and *explain*   These instructions remind you that the purpose of this piece of writing is to give information to somebody and to provide some practical suggestions of how to deal with difficulties.

- You have been given clear instructions as to the **form** of the task and the **audience** that you are addressing. The **tone** of your letter should be informal and appropriate to a younger relative.

- You should ensure that you conclude with a suitable valediction.

- You have been told to make your letter *lively* and *interesting* and have also been given the angle (that of someone who knows the ropes) from which to write it. You should, therefore, include not just **facts** but also some personal **comments** and **opinions** which convey 'insider' knowledge.

Extracts from Alice's Grade **C** answer

The beginning

Dear Natalie,

How are you and the rest of the family? Mum tells me that your mum says your a bit worried about starting at the new school so as I've had several years of experience of the place, I thought I'd give you some advise about how to survive here. It's really not too bad and don't forget you'll always have me to look after you.

GOOD POINTS

TONE AND FOCUS: Alice has shown a good grasp of the appropriate tone to use and has made a direct attempt to answer the question.

AWARENESS OF THE NEEDS OF THE READER: She has gone straight to the point so her reader is immediately involved in what she has to say.

TECHNICAL ACCURACY: Overall, her spelling and punctuation are quite secure, but she's made a couple of slips. Can you spot where they are?

IMPROVEMENTS NEEDED

► As an opening paragraph, this has a suitable tone and register, however, Alice could have given a little more thought to its structure. The final sentence contains two ideas which might have been better treated separately and she may have given herself a problem in making it link smoothly with what is to follow on.

► The spelling and punctuation slips are really due to carelessness; a higher grade piece of writing would avoid such errors although it might make others as a result of using more ambitious vocabulary, sentence structures, etc.

The middle

Alice's letter goes on to tell Natalie about the school and what she will be expected to do on the first day there. It contains quite a lot of useful information and gives a clear indication that she is writing from her expert knowledge of the school. This information is presented almost as a list, but in places it becomes a little muddled as the points aren't always carefully structured. Here is an extract:

The school is very big and you'll most probably get lost quite a lot. The science rooms are altogether at one end of the building and some of the science teachers can get really angry if you're not on time for their lessons. The gym is at the opposite end of the school and if you have science after PE it can take you a long time to get changed and then you'll be late and be given a detention if you're not carefull.

GOOD POINTS

USE OF RELEVANT EXAMPLES: Alice is continuing to write in an appropriately informal tone and has clearly identified a particular problem which her cousin might meet. Her inside knowledge of the science teachers is a helpful piece of information.

IMPROVEMENTS NEEDED

► CONTENT: Although the information that Alice gives is helpful, it's a little disjointed and there's no clear focus on the requirement to explain how to deal with the problem.

► STYLE: The sentence structures are accurate but rather repetitive. Alice should try varying the openings of the sentences instead of beginning each one in the same way. For example, she could start the last sentence like this: 'This can lead to a really big problem if you have Science straight after PE because...' in order to give some variety.

► STRUCTURE: The structure is rather loose. Alice has a tendency to put down ideas as they come into her head without selecting them or thinking about how best to order them. She could profitably spend some time planning ideas carefully before starting to write.

The ending

Well, I hope what I've written here will have given you some idea of what to watch out for and how to deal with problems when you come across them. In particular, remember what I've said about teachers. Most of them aren't that bad really and there human enough to understand if you've got problems. The important thing is not to be afraid to ask them and, remember, you've always got me to sort them out if things don't work out for you. I'll see you in September.

GOOD POINTS

LINKS: Alice has made a positive attempt to round off the letter with a **conclusion** which refers to and sums up the ideas which she's mentioned earlier.

TONE: Alice has maintained a consistently informal and friendly tone throughout the letter. Her sentence structures are more varied in the conclusion as well.

IMPROVEMENTS NEEDED

▶ **STRUCTURE:** There are several positive qualities in Alice's conclusion but there's a tendency to cram ideas together without developing them quite as fully as she could do. For example, her final point about her being there to sort things out isn't clear. Does she mean that she will sort out problems or teachers?

▶ **STYLE:** Those irritating spelling slips are still occurring and the letter would have been improved by including a correct valediction such as 'With love and best wishes' followed by Alice's name.

Typical exam question

Describe a dangerous place which is known to you and explain what makes it dangerous.
[20 marks]

What are the key words in this question?

● *Describe*   This tells you what the specific purpose of your writing is; you need to give **precise details** about the place: where and what it is; what it looks like, etc.

● *Explain*   You should give reasons based on your description as to why the place is dangerous.

● **You are not given a precise audience for your writing;** you should, therefore, assume that the audience is someone who does not know the place and requires particular details of it.

Extracts from Dan's Grade **A** answer

The beginning

I live near the seaside. Close by to me there is a famous beauty spot which is a high cliff jutting out into the sea. It is about 75 metres high and there is a precipitous drop on to the sharp rocks at its base; the sea boils and seethes around these rocks continuously and if anyone were to fall over the edge they would be caught up in the fierce maelstrom of eddying water and swiftly drowned – that is, if they survived the fall in the first place!

What makes this a good answer?

► There is a **direct opening** which gives a **clear focus** to the writing. Dan then goes on to elaborate on the opening statement by giving **precise details** and then a clear reason as to why the place is dangerous. By using the first person pronoun, 'I', Dan also makes it clear to the reader that the place is known to him.

► LANGUAGE: Dan has used precise and **original vocabulary** which is sophisticated in places. (Words such as 'seethes', 'fierce maelstrom of eddying water' are evidence that Dan has thought carefully about choosing **interesting descriptive words** to give a clear picture of what he is describing.)

► STYLE: Dan has varied his sentence structures effectively to make his writing interesting. He starts with a short, direct opening sentence which immediately involves the reader and then ends the paragraph with an involved complex sentence which describes the dangers and, incidentally, shows that he can use **sophisticated punctuation devices** such as the semi-colon and dash.

The middle – an outline plan

This type of writing needs to be carefully structured and organised. Dan has described the place as dangerous and now needs to go on and identify specific reasons as to what makes it particularly dangerous.

For example, he could describe what precautions are taken (if any) to prevent people falling over the edge. He needs to include a description of what the top of the cliff is like and the dangers it presents to different types of people (children, sightseers, etc.).

The ending

So, this place is dangerous for several reasons: it is an easily accessible beauty spot which is visited throughout the year by people of all ages from all walks of life. The safety precautions (a not particularly suitable wooden fence and some faded warning notices) are inadequate preventative measures either to restrain exuberant young children or to deter foolhardy adventurous types who want to go too close to the edge. Every year several people accidentally lose their lives here; there is clearly a need for the local authority to provide more effective safety measures, but perhaps they fear that if the element of danger is taken away its popularity may disappear. I know I would prefer to be able to visit and enjoy the beauty of the scenery without feeling my life was at risk and so would all my friends.

What makes this a good answer?

▶ **STRUCTURE:** This paragraph presents a **clear and focused conclusion** to the piece of writing. It gives clear evidence of being part of an overall plan and not only sums up what has gone before but concludes with a strong and fully relevant personal statement giving Dan's own point of view which clearly addresses his audience.

▶ **LINKS:** Dan begins with a connective, 'so', which relates directly back to his preceding paragraph and clearly introduces the summative points which will follow.

▶ **LANGUAGE:** Dan has continued to use **precise, appropriate and sophisticated vocabulary** ('inadequate preventative measures', 'restrain exuberant young children') and has shown that he can spell some potentially problematic words correctly.

▶ **STYLE:** Dan has continued to use some **complex sentence structures** and written consistently in a register which is both personal and informative, which is what this task requires.

Key skill: structuring your work

1

Organising your writing into carefully linked and logically connected paragraphs is an essential skill to use in this type of writing.

2

A carefully focused introductory statement is necessary to convey the main purpose of what you have to say to your reader.

3

Each paragraph you write should contain a topic sentence which encapsulates the main point which you are describing or explaining.

4

Your paragraphs should develop logically from each other; remember to use linking devices which indicate how they are connected.

5

There should be a clear sense of development of ideas throughout the piece of writing which culminates logically and inevitably in a concluding statement. An essay with a positive conclusion is a more impressive piece of writing than one which simply stops.

6

Even when working under time restrictions, it is a good idea to make a plan of your writing. This should not be too detailed, but writing out your topic sentences is a good approach; there is then something for the examiner to refer back to if, by any chance, you fail to finish in the time available.

7

As with all writing tasks it is important to show that you can vary your sentence structures to interest and involve the reader. The ability to use complex sentences with confidence is a clear indication of a writer who has a sophisticated control of English. There are three types of sentences; good writing uses a mixture of all three as appropriate:

– Simple sentences: I know a dangerous place. It is a very steep cliff. It is near where I live.

– Compound sentences (these are simple sentences made into one by the use of connectives): I know a dangerous place and it is a very steep cliff near where I live.

– Complex sentences (these are more grammatically sophisticated sentences which combine the simple sentences in a much tighter and more focused way): I know a dangerous place which is a very steep cliff, situated near to where I live.

DON'T
FORGET ...

✓ The **purpose** of this type of writing is to convey information; you must avoid the temptation to write a narrative.

✓ The reader will require **precise facts and details** to understand fully what you are describing or explaining.

✓ **Planning and structuring** your work is important; your paragraphs should be logically sequenced and organised and you should keep the requirements of your reader in mind at all times.

✓ Although you should use language appropriate to the task and remember that your main purpose is to provide information, you can still include some personal touches and opinions as long as they are suited to the task.

✓ The triplet 'inform, explain and describe' allows for a wide range of tasks to be set; some may be more factual than others. Make sure that you adapt the tone of voice you use in your writing to match the exact type of task you are answering.

What the examiners are looking for

To achieve a Grade C, your writing which aims to inform, explain or describe must:

1 Show you have a clear understanding of what you are writing about and the audience for whom you are writing.

You must show that you are clear as to the purpose of your writing and you must give evidence that you understand why your reader requires the information. It is a good idea, whenever possible, to base your information on your own knowledge and experience.

2 Be structured and clearly focused.

Your paragraphs should be linked both by content and through language (e.g. the use of connectives).

3 Interest and involve your reader.

You could do this by referring directly to your personal experiences and/or by addressing the reader directly to provide him or her with relevant information.

4 Be generally secure in spelling and punctuation.

This means that your spelling of straightforward vocabulary should be consistently accurate and that of more complex and ambitious words should be generally secure. To achieve a Grade C in a writing task, you should be confident in your use of full stops to separate sentences.

5 Show some variety of sentence structures and types.

There should be evidence that you can control some compound and complex sentences and that by doing so you can provide order and clarity in the information, explanations and descriptions that you give.

To achieve a Grade A, your writing which aims to inform, explain or describe must:

1 Use form, content and style which are consistently matched to audience and purpose.

Your writing should be clearly focused on the subject and contain a wide range of relevant and interesting details. You should show a clear understanding of the reader's specific requirements and subtlety in the way you present the material to meet these.

2 Show clear evidence of confident and sophisticated control of your material through structure and crafting.

Your writing should consistently show coherent and fluently linked sentence structures and paragraphs. You should show a varied range of ways of demonstrating information about the subject appropriate to your audience.

3 Show an extensive and original vocabulary range.

Your choice of words should be precise, appropriate to the task and interesting. At this level it is important that you show that you are in control of the words that you use and aren't just choosing the first ones to come into your head.

4 Use a wide range of punctuation with precision, contain correct spelling across a wide range of vocabulary and use a wide range and variety of sentence structures with purpose and precision.

Remember that it is your responsibility as a writer to show the examiner that you are in control of the structures and technicalities of writing English and that you are choosing those which are most suited to your purpose. An examiner can only reward what he or she can see!

Typical exam question

Write the words of a speech to be given to your year group at school in which you try to persuade them that to travel is better than to arrive.　　[20 marks]

What are the key words in this question?

- *Write the words of a speech*　You are being given the format of the task; you are therefore expected to show an awareness of this and make some attempt to use an **oral register** (but don't forget that you will be assessed on your writing skills).

- *Your year group*　You have also been given the **audience** for your speech; you should show an awareness of this in the content of your argument.

- *Persuade*　What you write must be convincing and you should show that you can use language and content in such a way that it will influence your audience into accepting your point of view.

Extracts from Chris's Grade C answer

The beginning

I think that there's a lot to be said for travelling and I'm sure that you'll agree with me. Last year I went with my family on holiday to the USA. Dad gave us the choice between staying in a fairly lively hotel in Florida or hiring a car and visiting different parts of the country. At first I wanted to stay in Florida as I thought that there would be loads of activities to do but everyone else wanted to hire the car and now that we've done it I'm very glad that we did.

GOOD POINTS

OPENING: Chris has written a direct, clearly focused opening which relates directly to the question and is likely to attract and hold the attention of the reader.

IDEAS AND STRUCTURE: There is a clear indication of the direction which the essay is going to take (although it may become unnecessarily anecdotal).

EXPRESSION AND ACCURACY: What Chris has written is a direct treatment of the question, written in an accurate if unambitious way. Although the sentence structures are somewhat limited, they are accurately expressed with no immediately apparent errors.

IMPROVEMENTS NEEDED

▶ **EXPRESSION:** Although the opening has some good colloquial vocabulary, it lacks the overall register of a formal speech.

▶ **STRUCTURE AND FOCUS:** There's a suspicion that the essay could go off at a tangent; Chris has introduced his family holiday but there's no indication that the essay will continue to focus clearly on the benefits of travelling; there's a possibility that it might turn into another of those 'What I did on my summer holidays' pieces of writing. To avoid this Chris should:

– decide on how he intends to conclude the essay

– keep his conclusion in mind to ensure staying on task

– make a plan of the main points he will make in order to reach that conclusion

– remember that each of these points should be developed on in order to produce a fully coherent and convincing argument.

The middle

It was in the middle of the second week that I realised why I enjoyed travelling. We had visited several exciting places such as the Grand Canyon. We had also been to a couple of big and exciting towns. We had seen a lot of different scenery. I realised that I wouldn't have seen as much if we had stayed in one place.

GOOD POINTS

RELEVANCE: This paragraph is clearly linked to the topic and is well placed to explain Chris's response to the task.

IMPROVEMENTS NEEDED

▶ **REGISTER:** Although the content is relevant to the task, Chris is writing in a narrative register. It would help to adopt a more consistently oral tone.

▶ **STRUCTURE:** The explanation of why he enjoys travelling is clearly conveyed but it reads a little like a conclusion. Chris may find it difficult to develop the argument from this point without repeating himself.

▶ **SENTENCE STRUCTURE:** The sentences are accurately expressed and correctly punctuated. However, there is a lack of variation in their openings; more variety would improve the grade.

The ending

So, by the end of the holiday I'd seen more than I'd ever dreamed of. I have a lot of interesting memories and they mean a lot to me. I told my Dad that I was glad that he suggested the idea. When you travel from place to place you have a great sense of freedom and you don't have to do what other people want. I got a lot of enjoyment from wondering what the places would be like which we drove to and I can definitely say that I enjoyed going to them as much or more than arriving.

GOOD POINTS

CONTENT: Chris has kept focused on his argument and gives good reasons for holding his opinion.

CONCLUSION: Chris has made a positive attempt to refer to the topic in his concluding paragraph and has summed up his argument quite effectively.

ACCURACY: Chris's expression is accurate and his tone has been consistent throughout the essay.

IMPROVEMENTS NEEDED

▶ **FOCUS ON TASK:** Although Chris has produced a consistently developed argument, he has not paid much attention to the need to persuade which is one of the key requirements of the question. He has relied on his argument convincing people rather than using any specific persuasive linguistic devices.

▶ **EXPRESSION AND TONE:** Chris's tone is rather passive and descriptive; he has been asked to write the words of a speech and a greater indication that he is aware of ways of communicating dramatically and effectively with his target audience would be to his advantage.

Typical exam question

'The younger generation see reading as a thing of the past; we should close down libraries and turn them into internet centres.'

Argue your point of view about this statement. [20 marks]

What are the key words in this question?

- *Argue your point of view* You have not been given a specific audience for this task so you should address your ideas to the examiner, who is the reader. *Argue* suggests that you should construct a logical (and persuasive) piece of writing. *Your point of view* means that you can take either aspect of the statement to write about and that your argument need not be balanced. A good response is likely to show an appreciation of the points of view of both sides, however.

Extract's from Mary's Grade **A** answer

The beginning

And why shouldn't we do so? Is there really any point in maintaining these draughty, unwelcoming places with their dull rows of shelves all creaking under the weight of dry and crumbling volumes which give off clouds of dust and pollute the atmosphere? Far better, I suggest, to throw their musty contents on to the rubbish heap and refurbish their newly naked insides with bank upon bank of glittering screens passively awaiting the influx of eager technokids bursting with excitement to acquire the latest crumbs of knowledge which the world wide web can offer or to pass their valuable free time in downloading and playing the latest version of Rampant Racing Road Rage Turtles!

What makes this a good answer?

▶ **READER INVOLVEMENT:** Mary **begins with questions**. The first is short and sharp; the second longer and more complex. The reader is immediately involved by this confident opening.

▶ **VOCABULARY AND SENTENCE STRUCTURES:** Mary's **vocabulary is wide and original** and clearly suggests an enjoyment in writing. **There is a good and varied range of sentence structures and types** which keeps the reader interested.

▶ **TONE AND PURPOSE:** Apparently the content of this opening paragraph suggests that Mary is adopting a **deliberately challenging and controversial approach** to the topic which is likely to provoke a response from the reader; however, there are sufficient hints in her choice of vocabulary and in the rather overstated way in which some of the comments are expressed to suggest to the reader that perhaps she may be about to present a more conventional viewpoint in an original way.

Extract from the middle

In the white heat of our technologically-challenged world, the younger generation have no need or time to engage in the quiet and reflective pleasures to be gained by sitting in a comfortable armchair and allowing themselves to be transported into the world of the imagination created for them by writers such as Dickens and Jane Austen. No, it is far better for them to watch scenes of excitement and violence played out before their eyes as they are involved in the latest adventures presented to them by the great range of reality TV shows available for their consumption; the effort involved in using their imagination and engaging in the demanding and tiring task of thinking, is immediately removed.

What makes this a good answer?

▶ **DEVELOPMENT:** This shows a consistent development in tone and attitude from the opening. Mary's **ironic approach** to her topic is becoming clearly and effectively apparent.

▶ **CONTROL:** The writer is clearly **in control** both of her argument and in the way she is **manipulating her reader** into sharing her point of view.

▶ **LANGUAGE:** The language used is fully appropriate to the content; the **use of the semi-colon to balance the final sentence** and to throw emphasis on the latter part of it is particularly effective.

The ending

> So, in conclusion, what, may I ask, are the important values which should be instilled into us, the younger generation? Should we be passively fed with pre-digested entertainment and information which we can obtain at the push of a button or the click of a mouse or should we be encouraged or even forced into making the effort to research and evaluate information for ourselves, even if it means exercising our minds in order to do so? Do we really want our brains to become stagnant? A world run by machines may offer comfort and ease but what would our future be if the machines ever break down and no-one knows how or where to find the information to repair them? Libraries, and the books they contain, must be preserved.

What makes this a good answer?

► **STRUCTURE:** Mary has **sustained her approach and tone** throughout the essay but has acknowledged her conclusion by emphasising strongly what her real opinion is and leaving the reader with a forceful statement of it.

► **PERSUASIVE LANGUAGE:** The response shows a very clear awareness of the need to argue and persuade and the **series of rhetorical questions** with which this conclusion begins is a very effective way of influencing the reader into sharing the writer's point of view.

► **RHETORIC:** What makes Mary's conclusion particularly powerful is the **control she shows over the rhythms of her sentences** which involve and convince the reader of the truth of their argument.

Key skill: structuring your argument

1

With anything you write, your **thoughts must be effectively connected** to help your readers follow your ideas and understand exactly what you are thinking.

2

Your vocabulary needs to be precise and carefully chosen; try to ensure that you can choose the right word to produce exactly the response you want from your readers.

3

Your sentences should be clear and complete units of sense and be logically linked to each other through the use of appropriate connectors such as therefore, however, nevertheless, etc.

4

In particular, you should pay careful attention to your paragraphing. Each paragraph should focus on a particular idea, be structured around a topic sentence and be linked to the paragraphs which precede and follow it. When you are planning your writing it's a good idea to **use topic sentences to provide the skeleton of your ideas.**

5

In all your writing, but particularly that to argue, persuade or advise, **opening and concluding paragraphs are especially important.** Your opening paragraph should involve your reader and give a clear indication of the direction your writing is taking; your conclusion should sum up all that has been said and refer back to the main point of your introduction. Remember, there's a great difference between a piece of writing which concludes with a well-planned and focused ending and a piece which just finishes because the writer has no more to say.

DON'T FORGET ...

✓ The purpose of your writing is to argue, persuade or advise. This means that you must try to **convince an audience** to believe or do something.

✓ You will need to show that you have a **confident grasp of your subject**, so you should **support your argument with facts and evidence**.

✓ Make sure that your tone and register match the demands of the task: *advise* means that your writing should be convincingly supported by facts; *argue* requires you to **present considered opinions**.

✓ Always **keep the audience of your writing clearly in mind**; you can argue much more effectively if you do this.

✓ The **structure** of your writing is particularly important; **plan and organise** your ideas thoughtfully and make sure that you have a **striking opening and convincing conclusion**.

✓ The purpose of your writing is to convince your audience of something; in order to do so, your **language must be precise** and you should show a clear awareness of how to use **the power of words** to influence the emotions of your readers by using humour or anger, for example.

What the examiners are looking for

To achieve a Grade C, your writing which aims to argue, persuade or advise must:

1 Clearly present the writer's point of view.

Show a **clear understanding of the purpose of your writing** and be consistent in the way you construct and present your ideas.

2 Keep closely to the format required by the task.

Pay particular attention to what the task tells you about **the audience and format of your writing**; if you are required to write the words of the speech, you should show the examiner that you have an awareness of the need to use an oral register. Beginning your writing with a statement such as 'Fellow students…' is a simple but effective way to do this.

3 Show an ordered and logical development of ideas.

Your writing should be **paragraphed** and show **evidence of planning and structure**. There should be a clear indication that your **paragraphs are linked** and that you have given some thought to how your points follow on one from another.

4 Show some variety of sentence structures and vocabulary.

You should show that you have an appreciation of how **varying your sentence structures and vocabulary** can be used to influence your readers to gain the effects you want. For example, short sentences can be used to emphasise a point and thinking carefully about your choice of words is an extremely important way to create a response in your reader.

5 Be secure in punctuation and spelling.

You should show that you are capable of being able to **use punctuation devices effectively to help shape your meaning**; in particular, you should be confident in using full stops to separate sentences. In order to produce the required response from your readers you cannot afford any possibility that they may lose track of what you are saying through failure to punctuate or spell correctly.

To achieve a Grade A, your writing which aims to argue, persuade or advise must:

1 Contain confidently and convincingly presented views.

You should show that you are **fully in control of your arguments** and that what you write is knowledgeable, informed and clearly aware of the need to persuade or convince an audience. Your writing should be **clearly focused on the question** and the content should be varied, interesting and relevant.

2 Closely observe the required format.

Read the question carefully and ensure that your writing consistently follows the format of the task in register and tone.

3 Be effectively and logically structured.

Show that you have clearly thought through and planned your writing. **Paragraphs should be logically structured** and expressed cogently and coherently.

4 Show a varied and controlled range of sentence structures and vocabulary.

Show that you have both the vocabulary to communicate the range and complexity of your thoughts and the ability to convey them convincingly **through complex sentence structures which will engage and control the reader's response to what you have written.**

5 Show controlled and accurate spelling and punctuation.

You must show that you are in **complete control of punctuation and the spelling of the words** you use. Writing which deserves a Grade A mark should use a varied and sophisticated vocabulary and the spelling of this should be accurate. (Examiners will allow a few slips, however!) Punctuation should be fully secure and used positively to produce the required responses from your reader. In particular, you should show that you are **confident in using the more sophisticated punctuation devices such as the semi-colon.**

Typical exam question

'Nearly all popular TV programmes are mindless entertainment; they are no more than moving wallpaper.'

'Popular TV programmes reflect real life and help the viewers to understand the world of which they are part.'

Analyse one of the statements above and, by referring to one or two TV programmes, comment on how far you think it can be justified.

[20 marks]

What are the key words in this question?

- *Analyse*   *Analyse* means to break something down into its component parts. You should, therefore, indicate that you have a good understanding of all the implications of the statement about which you are writing.

- *Referring to one or two TV programmes* You need to write in detail about **actual examples to support your analysis**; make sure that you choose programmes about which you have sufficient knowledge to write convincingly.

- *Comment*   This means that after you've considered your chosen programme(s), you should state how they help you to **justify the point** you are making.

Extracts from Jayne's Grade **C** answer

The beginning

I think television programmes tell us alot about real life, my family watch programmes like Casualty and The Bill and we all agree that their full of people you can believe in who do real things.

Take Casualty for example. You can learn a lot about what happens in hospital emergancy departments and realise that the doctors and nurses are just the same as ordinary people with their own personal problems and worries. You also learn quite alot about operations and different illnesses and some of the things they show might help if you ever needed to give first aid to someone who was in trouble. It also helps you to understand the problems hospitals have with finding enough money to keep them going.

GOOD POINTS

FOCUS ON TASK: Jayne has shown a good understanding of what the task requires and has made her position clear in her opening paragraph.

ARGUMENTS: Jayne's second paragraph, in particular, shows that she has some relevant ideas and points to make about this topic.

IMPROVEMENTS NEEDED

► STRUCTURE: Although what Jayne has written shows that she has some good ideas about the topic and has chosen some relevant examples, they could be more carefully structured. The ideas appear to be written down just as she thinks of them rather than being logically ordered. A better response would treat the different ideas in her second paragraph separately and develop each of them into a paragraph of its own.

► AWARENESS OF GENRE: Although Jayne is writing about specific programmes as requested, there could definitely be a more analytical approach in the way she treats them.

► EXPRESSION: There are some spelling mistakes of basic vocabulary and on one occasion a comma has been used to separate sentences rather than a full stop. Jayne has also forgotten to place the names of the television programmes within inverted commas. Overall, her vocabulary and sentence structures are quite sound but unexciting and too many slips like those mentioned could easily reduce her grade.

The middle

So as I've said, Casualty helps us to understand what goes on in hospitals today. Sometimes you might think that to much happens at once in the same episode. For example, there is nearly always someone who has a rare disease which is only cured at the end of the programme and there is always a surprising number of road accidents and other such matters. Usualy, in the final episode of a series something spectatular happens such as the hospital is attacked by suicide bombers or one of the main characters is killed off or accused of doing something wrong. This is a bit far-fetched and not always like real life but it does show you how people cope in an emergency and also reminds you that nobody is perfect or lives forever.

GOOD POINTS

RELEVANCE: Jayne has continued to keep closely focused on the task. She is making some relevant comments and criticisms about the television programme and is also giving some reasons to support these comments.

STRUCTURE: This paragraph sums up the first section of Jayne's essay and relates it back to the topic. She is now in a position to move on to comment on another television series and has left herself several options by which she can link into her next paragraph.

EXPRESSION: Overall, Jayne's sentences show some variation of length and she has not repeated the sentence separation error which occurred in her opening paragraph. The ability to use full stops consistently correctly is one of the main features which distinguishes Grade C from Grade D writing.

IMPROVEMENTS NEEDED

▶ **DEVELOPMENT OF IDEAS:** Jayne is clearly an intelligent candidate who makes some perceptive comments about the television series. However, she has a tendency to state a criticism and then move on to another. It would help to improve her grade if she were to devote some more time to developing and explaining the points she makes in greater detail.

▶ **MATCHING STYLE TO CONTENT:** Jayne writes fluently and apart from the occasional slip in spelling and punctuation, her work is accurate. However, the register she uses is somewhat colloquial and as a result comes over as quite limited. A more sophisticated use of language and a slightly more objective tone would improve the impression she gives.

The conclusion

So, after considering two popular TV series, we can agree that popular television programmes do reflect real life. Both series contain characters who are convincing and could easily be members of your family or your next door neighbours. This makes you realise that people like doctors, nurses and policemen are real people with ordinary worries and problems. The reason we think this is because the acting in the programmes is good and because the storeys are well written. Both series show us life as it really is, they dont set out to make things more attractive than they really are and so we can believe in what they show and imagine how we would behave in the same situation. Their not like some films, such as Spiderman which has got nothing to do with real life at all.

GOOD POINTS

SUMMING UP: In some ways, this paragraph is the best part of Jayne's essay. She has drawn her ideas together well and has allowed herself time to comment on them.
EXPLANATIONS: Jayne has made some sensible points about why these television programmes are convincing and has justified them by giving reasons as to why she thinks so.

IMPROVEMENTS NEEDED

▶ FOCUS AND STRUCTURE: As already mentioned, this is a good concluding paragraph but it could still be tidied up and focused more tightly. The final sentence is not necessary and gives the impression of being an afterthought. Jayne should either have developed it into a separate paragraph or omitted it altogether. The final sentence is always important, as it leaves a lasting impression in the examiner's mind.

▶ EXPRESSION: Jayne's written expression is of a consistent standard. As already mentioned, a little more variety and sophistication would help. As a general rule, Grade C writing is accurate but lacking in range and variety. Once examiners become aware of more variety in sentence structure and vocabulary, then they start to think of the highest grades.

Extracts from Leroy's Grade **A** answer

The beginning

British-made television soap operas certainly set out to reflect the lives of real people and to deal with issues which are of concern to their viewers. However, it should be remembered that they are produced not with a sociological purpose, but with the intention of attracting and entertaining more viewers than those of similar programmes on rival channels. So, although the first half of the statement can be quite easily proved to be true, the second part, as to how far these programmes help viewers to understand their own lives, needs greater consideration. Although the success of soaps depends on presenting characters living recognisably ordinary lives, it does not necessarily mean that viewers identify and empathise with them on more than a superficial level. In order to consider this point further it is necessary to look closely at some specific examples.

What makes this a good answer?

▶ **EXPLANATION:** Leroy has made a **strong opening statement** in which he indicates a mature understanding of the implications of the statement about which he is writing and clearly **indicates the direction** his comments will take.

▶ **STRUCTURE:** Leroy has decided to focus his response on TV soaps; this means that he has avoided the temptation to make too many unsupported generalised comments and has **developed his argument** in such a way that he can move smoothly on to **considering specific examples** in the following paragraphs.

▶ **REGISTER:** As this is a topic which requires an objective approach, Leroy has appropriately decided to write in **an impersonal register** (e.g. 'it does not mean') which gives a more convincing effect than using the personal pronoun, 'I'.

▶ **LANGUAGE:** Leroy has used a **mature and sophisticated vocabulary** which is appropriate to the task (e.g. 'empathise'; 'superficial'). His spelling of potentially problematic words (e.g. 'recognisably') is accurate and he is confidently **using complex sentence structures to convey the complex ideas** which he is expressing.

The middle

Most British-made soaps present recognisable characters living in a convincing background and this is enough to allow their audiences to identify with the characters' attitude and concerns. It should not be necessary to live in the north-west of England or to have been born within the sound of Bow bells to share the worlds of "Coronation Street" and "Eastenders" respectively. What is important is that the fictional characters who inhabit these worlds experience the same emotions and problems as those of viewers of the same age group and gender. This sense of identification is important in other ways too as it is an important means whereby families are drawn together and encouraged to share their problems. Soaps provide genuine family viewing as they are watched by different generations of the family together. I always watch soaps with my parents and sister, and even my grandparents if they are visiting.

What makes this a good answer?

► **TOPIC SENTENCE:** Leroy's opening sentence clearly **signals the main point of the paragraph** and provides plenty of opportunity for development and explanation of this point.

► **ANALYTICAL TONE:** Leroy is continuing to write in an objective, impersonal tone to create a **scientific, analytical register** which helps to make his comments sound convincing.

► **DEVELOPMENT:** Towards the end of the paragraph, Leroy introduces a **refinement of his topic sentence point** (the reference to soaps as family viewing), **which will enable him to develop this idea further** in the next paragraph.

The conclusion

In conclusion, it can be said that soaps are a valuable means of helping people come to terms with their own experiences and those of their family members. This is largely due to the skills with which the programmes are researched, scripted and acted. The audiences believe in the characters in the programmes as they can recognise them as being just like themselves, suffering from similar trivial but personally important problems. In my opinion, it is only when the plot lines become over-sensational (for example, when a character turns out to be a serial killer) or over-didactic (such as when a public moral issue such as abortion is dealt with in a somewhat self-conscious way) that the programmes lose their basis in real life and become no more than mere entertainment; in general, however, this seldom happens and a large number of viewers from all walks of life benefit from what they can offer.

What makes this a good answer?

▶ **ANALYTICAL APPROACH:** Leroy has considered the various implications of the topic and weighed them up through looking at specific examples, but, at the same time, has indicated that there are not necessarily any right or wrong conclusions to be drawn. All he has done is to **show a keen awareness of the possible interpretations.**

▶ **DRAWING POINTS TOGETHER:** There is a positive sense of conclusion in Leroy's final paragraph. He is showing that this is a point at which he definitely plans to finish his essay and has **drawn together the main points** he has made earlier.

▶ **STRUCTURE:** Leroy's conclusion shows an awareness of two very important techniques: he has brought up reference to the opening of his essay to show a completeness to his thinking but has also introduced a new idea which, although complete in itself, nevertheless leaves the way open for further consideration and indicates his **understanding of the analytical processes.**

Key skill: writing for different purposes and audiences

1

First of all, consider the key words in a writing task, for example, *analyse*, *inform* or *persuade*. These words are central to telling what the purpose of your writing is to be and you should think about the appropriate language to use to create the required effect on your reader. For example, you will use a different type of language depending upon your purpose:

- *analyse* means that you are likely to use a rather objective tone as analysis is a scientific process and your writing should convey a balanced and thoughtful approach; you may use abstract terms and a speculative approach which could be reflected in complex sentence structures and the use of questions;

- *inform* means that your writing should be less complex; your concern is to convey some information as clearly as possible and you should use simple, clear vocabulary and sentence structures so that the reader can concentrate on what is being said rather than how you are saying it;

- *persuade* suggests that you wish to make your readers share your viewpoint even though initially they may not want to; you are likely to use rhetorical devices in your writing such as many questions which lead the reader to only one possible answer (that is, the one you want) and emotive language which will help to influence the reader's emotional response.

2

At all times you must keep your audience in mind and think about what they are already likely to know and how to choose the appropriate vocabulary and tone of voice to involve them in what you are writing; you would need to adopt a different approach if you were giving information to your headteacher from what you would use if talking to a friend.

Key skill: presenting an overview

1

You should attempt to show an overall understanding of the main implications of the issues about which you are writing.

2

This type of writing involves showing an awareness of the possible different interpretations and judgements that can be made about your chosen topic.

3

Follow through your different ideas and try to balance them together; it is likely that your conclusion will draw from them rather than finishing with simply accepting one to the exclusion of all others.

4

In order to show your overall understanding you need to try to make connections and relationships between apparently different ideas.

5

Remember that you need to give examples and provide evidence to support your comments. It is a good idea to keep to examples which are within your own experience.

DON'T FORGET ...

✓ Writing to analyse, review or comment means that you should show an **awareness of the different ways a topic can be considered**; it is important that you indicate to the examiner your appreciation of the importance of this.

✓ Once you have considered different interpretations of a topic, you should weigh up the validity of each one; your language should reflect this (e.g. 'on the other hand'; 'however, it can be argued...', etc.).

✓ You should not just review and consider different ideas but also follow them through to consider **how effectively they support your overall judgements** about your chosen topic.

✓ In particular, try to show that you can **make connections between the different points of view** and examples which you have considered; this is a way of showing how perceptive your thinking is; if you can follow through connections in the implications of different ideas, you are doing this at quite a high level and will be rewarded for original thinking.

✓ You should try to show that you have some **knowledge of the topic about which you are writing** by using examples and evidence to support the abstract points that you are making.

What the examiners are looking for

To achieve a Grade C, your writing which aims to analyse, review or comment must:

1 Be supported by appropriate and relevant examples.

These can be used to illustrate your analytical comments.

2 Present a clear overview of the task.

You should relate this to the reader through a **consistent tone and appropriate vocabulary**.

3 Give a clear indication of your intended approach in the opening.

This should then develop in some detail to a **sensible and focused conclusion**.

4 Be organised into paragraphs of varying length which help to shape and convey meaning to the reader.

These paragraphs should be **linked by straightforward connectives**. The spelling of commonly used vocabulary should be secure and punctuation should be used generally to clarify meaning.

To achieve a Grade A, your writing which aims to analyse, review or comment must:

1 Show a sharply focused perceptive insight into the topic.

This can be achieved by **detailed analysis of specific examples** supported by **relevant and appropriate personal comment**.

2 Show a complete grasp of the topic.

Explore it thoroughly, revealing a **varied tone and fully appropriate and sophisticated technical vocabulary**.

3 Show a very effective opening which engages directly with the topic.

This should develop into a fully coherent and sustained development and lead to a **convincing and balanced conclusion**. Paragraphs should show skilful construction and be purposefully varied in length, and linked through a range of connectives and connective devices which reinforce **a sense of cohesion in your argument**.

4 Be expressed through varied and elaborated sentence structures.

Spelling of a wide range of vocabulary should be fully correct (although a few slips are acceptable). There should be a good range of punctuation correctly and positively used to create specific effects.

NON-FICTION TEXTS

This is not intended to be a complete paper. What follows are three articles which are representative of the sort of articles you will meet in your exam and a range of questions on them. If you try answering all the questions, you will be practising all the skills and techniques you will need (whichever specification you are following).

Question 1

1   **Read Item 1, *Nightmare of the Grey Goo*. You are being asked to distinguish between fact and opinion.**

   Choose 3 opinions. Write each down and explain how you know each is an opinion and not a fact.   [6 marks]

2   **Read Item 2, *Tiny robots with massive potential*. You are being asked to select material appropriate to purpose.**

   Explain, using your own words, what the article tells you about nanotechnology and advantages and problems which could arise from it.   [10 marks]

3   **Compare Item 1 with Item 2 and identify similarities and differences.**

   Compare:
   ● what they have to say
   ● the language used to say it.   [10 marks]

4   **Read Item 1, *Nightmare of the Grey Goo* and Item 3, *Who will control the nanobots?* Compare how the writers of both articles express their concerns over nanotechnology.**

   In your answer you should look closely at how the articles use presentation, content and language.   [20 marks]

Item 1

Nightmare of the Grey Goo

PRINCE CHARLES has warned that life on Earth could be wiped out by scientists 'playing God' with potentially lethal new technologies.

The Mail on Sunday has learned that the Prince has summoned experts to a crisis summit over fears that the planet could be engulfed in a so-called 'grey goo catastrophe' caused by experiments going wrong.

The campaign reflects his continuing concern over environmental issues following his successful crusade in highlighting the dangers of genetically modified food, and centres on nano-technology, the cutting-edge new science that involves meddling with molecules and atoms that make up the universe.

His intervention last night set him on a collision course with the Government, which has given its full support to scientists involved in this controversial research, claiming it could be worth a fortune for British industry.

Tony Blair himself has described nanoscience as 'startling in its potential'.

But Charles won powerful support from Britain's best-known Green campaigner, Jonathon Porritt, who said: 'This research has radical consequences and we need to be much more alert about its implications.'

The row follows claims by some experts that nanotechnology could spark a freak accident – the so-called 'grey goo' nightmare – where tiny nanobots could gobble up the Earth.

Environmentalists deny it is science fiction fantasy and say it could happen if governments fail to impose strict controls on maverick scientists.

Enthusiasts say nanotechnology could create new miracle light-weight materials, cures for deadly diseases and super-fast microchips. Research is already taking place at some of Britain's most prestigious universities including Oxford and Cambridge.

The Americans see the potential of the technology for new defence equipment – including body-armour and light-weight fighting vehicles.

If the Prince continues to oppose Government policy, he risks a constitutional crisis. While he is free to vent his views on 'non-political' issues, such as modern architecture, as a member of the Royal Family he is forbidden from going head-to-head with the Government on matters of public policy.

Charles's worries were triggered by old-Etonian environmental campaigner Zac Goldsmith, who is emerging as one of the Prince's most important advisers.

Mr Goldsmith, editor of *The Ecologist* magazine, defended the Prince's decision to get involved in the row.

'He can play an enormously important role in leading the debate,' he said. 'The potential is there for the grey goo effect. It is a Pandora's box.

'With nanotechnology there is massive room for disaster. It is quite terrifying that there has been no debate on this issue. Some people may say the genie is out of the bottle already.

'But in fact it will only be pushed out of the bottle with billions of pounds of research money. There is still time to ask if we are wise enough as a species to handle this new technology.'

The Big Down report, published earlier this year by the Canadian-based ECT Group, is seen by ecologists as the definitive work on nanotechnology.

The survey recommends an international agreement restricting nanotech research. It also warns that even if the grey goo nightmare proves to be unfounded, nanotech poses other threats to the planet.

For example, it argues, some of the new miracle materials could have unforeseen side-effects – rather like asbestos, once hailed as a wonder-substance, which was later revealed to pose deadly risks.

Ottilia Saxl, chief executive of the Stirling-based Institute of Nanotechnology said the new technology would bring huge benefits.

'There are great prospects, particularly in medical research. This is not about unlocking a Pandora's box. The idea of self-replicating nanorobots is pure science fiction,' she said. 'You cannot regulate every aspect of nanotechnology. We need to have a commonsense approach.'

Item 2

Tiny robots with massive potential

Mail on Sunday Reporter

THE concept of nano-technology was first suggested by legendary US physicist Richard Feynman more than 40 years ago when he predicted the future thrust of technology would not be to build large machines, but incredibly small ones.

However, it was not until 1990 that the new science had a real breakthrough. A team of IBM researchers managed to manipulate 35 individual atoms so that they spelled out 'IBM'.

At its simplest, nano-technology is technology on the scale of a billionth of a metre or about 100,000th of the width of the human hair. It is science on the level of individual atoms and molecules – and it is only recently that microscopes powerful enough to study these basic materials of matter have been developed.

This new technology allows scientists for the first time to move around and, crucially, alter the individual building blocks that make up the universe.

Already experts have produced a powerful microchip just one millimetre across – so small it can be held in the mandible of an ant. Another breakthrough has been a tiny pill-sized submarine with a camera that, when swallowed, can spot internal bleeding or tumours.

However, most of the potential benefits – and risks – lie in the future. Experts say it will enable the development of artificial substances which could lead to ultra-lightweight aircraft or 'smart' bandages for faster healing. And according to nanotech's enthusiasts, even this is just the beginning. The next step would be to create 'universal assemblers': tiny robots or 'nanobots' that can be programmed to build just about anything, atom by atom, from the raw materials. In theory this would allow the manufacture of aircraft or cars that are 100 per cent perfect. Experts believe the first prototype nanobots could be developed by 2010.

There is another step envisaged by the nanotech scientists. They want to build more efficient nanobots that could make copies of themselves – to reproduce like bacteria. This is, in essence, what life does. A tree sucks air and water out of its environment and uses the power of sunlight to turn them into wood.

Scientists claim a self-replicating nanobot could 'feed' in a bucket of iron, sand or wood and in an hour it might make a trillion copies of itself.

But what if a nanobot fails to stop replicating itself? Doom-mongers warn that a mutant strain of these tiny robots could escape to a laboratory and begin 'feeding' on the matter around them. This is where the 'grey goo' theory comes in.

There are fears that these technologies could run wildly out of control. In the worst case scenario, the entire planet could be engulfed, the nanobots leaving behind nothing but a formless 'grey goo'.

Scientists disagree about whether we will ever be able to develop these self-replicating robots, although some believe the concept will be a reality in just ten or 20 years.

Item 3

MY SUMMER holiday reading last year included Michael Crichton's book, *Prey*.

It's an entertaining bit of nonsense about a group of ruthless scientists working on a high-tech military contract who accidentally end up releasing a swarm of self-replicating, man-eating 'nanoparticles' into the Nevada desert.

The hero scientist just manages to save us all from global catastrophe. So prepare to be sort-of scared when the film comes out later this year.

To get your head round all this nano stuff, you have to think very small indeed. Imagine a length of cloth one metre long, and then slice it up into a billion fragments. Each of those would be one nanometre wide. A human hair is about 100,000 nanometres wide.

So how can anyone be talking about technologies operating at such an impossibly small scale? Astonishingly powerful microscopes now allow scientists to manipulate materials at the atomic level, atom by atom. And they're well on the way to building tiny robots (nanobots!) to carry out assembly work following sophisticated computer programmes.

That means there's already a lot of money going into nanotechnology – from governments (there's nearly £2 billion of global government expenditure per annum) and big business.

Britain has a reasonably good record in nanoscience, and the DTI has committed around £50 million to support a new UK strategy for Nanotechnology.

Some people see it as the most important breakthrough since the wheel; others believe it threatens the end of life as we know it.

Here's a classic bit of nano-hype from Mark Modzelewski, director of the Nanobusiness Alliance: 'The importance of nanotechnology to the future of mankind cannot be overstated. Nanotech's promise is clean industries, cures for disease,

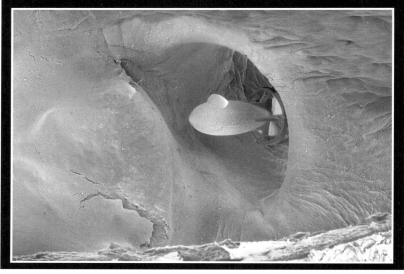

Who will control the nanobots?

nearly unlimited energy supplies and perhaps the end of hunger.'

Erich Drexler, the 'father' of nanotechnology, enthuses about the potential for nanobots to whiz around cleaning up pollution we cause, or to 'cohabit' inside our bodies, eliminating cancers or prolonging life indefinitely.

On the other side of the divide are the prophets of doom. Bill Joy, of Sun Microsystems, conjures up a world in which nanobots get out of control, breaking everything down into a 'grey goo' in an uninhabitable wasteland.

And what if these technologies fell into the wrong hands, with weapons of mass destruction being superseded by weapons of nano-destruction?

Current reality is more prosaic than these scenarios. Some sun-screens now use nano-sized zinc oxide particles, and cosmetics company L'Oréal markets anti-ageing 'nanocreams' that it claims work by getting deep down into the skin. And a vast number of new developments are in the pipeline. The number of new patents (civil and military) rises steeply every year.

So should we celebrate the genius of our scientists – or gear up for public protests to stop the nano-juggernaut in its tracks?

I haven't a clue. As an environmentalist, I find the potential for reducing pollution and increasing the efficiency with which we use natural resources exciting.

If it is possible to revolutionise solar cell technology or grow products atom by atom, clean up our contaminated land or nuclear waste, then I'd have to be a curmudgeon to look this gift horse in the mouth. All I do know right now is that we have to engineer a far more engaged public debate about such world-shaking technologies. And we would surely be well advised to proceed with a great deal more caution and forethought than is currently the case.

By Jonathon Porritt

POETRY FROM DIFFERENT CULTURES

Question 2

Compare the ways in which the poets of *Night of the scorpion* and *Vultures* use living creatures in their poems.

[20 marks]

Night of the scorpion

I remember the night my mother
was stung by a scorpion. Ten hours
of steady rain had driven him
to crawl beneath a sack of rice
Parting with his poison – flash
of diabolic tail in the dark room –
he risked the rain again.
The peasants came like swarms of flies
and buzzed the name of God a hundred times
to paralyse the Evil One.
With candles and with lanterns
throwing giant scorpion shadows
on the mud-baked walls
They searched for him: he was not found.
They clicked their tongues.
With every movement that the scorpion made
His poison moved in mother's blood, they said.
May he sit still, they said.
May the sins of your previous birth
be burned away tonight, they said.

May your suffering decrease
The misfortunes of your next birth, they said.
May the sum of evil
balanced in this unreal world
against the sum of good
become diminished by your pain.
May the poison purify your flesh
of desire, and your spirit of ambition,
they said, and they sat around
on the floor with my mother in the centre,
the peace of understanding on each face.
More candles, more lanterns, more neighbours,
more insects, and the endless rain.
My mother twisted through and through,
groaning on a mat.
My father, sceptic, rationalist,
trying every curse and blessing,
powder, mixture, herb and hybrid.
He even poured a little paraffin
Upon the bitten toe and put a match to it.
I watched the flame feeding on my mother.
I watched the holy man perform his rites
to tame the poison with an incantation.
After twenty hours
it lost its sting.

My mother only said
Thank God the scorpion picked on me
and spared my children.

Nissim Ezekiel

Vultures

In the greyness
and drizzle of one despondent
dawn unstirred by harbingers
of sunbreak a vulture
perching high on broken
bone of a dead tree
nestled close to his
mate his smooth
bashed-in head, a pebble
on a stem rooted in
a dump of gross
feathers, inclined affectionately
to hers. Yesterday they picked
the eyes of a swollen
corpse in a water-logged
trench and ate the
things in its bowel. Full
gorged they chose their roost
keeping the hollowed remnant
in easy range of cold
telescopic eyes…
Strange
indeed how love in other
ways so particular
will pick a corner
in that charnel-house
tidy it and coil up there, perhaps
even fall asleep – her face
turned to the wall!

…Thus the Commandant at Belsen
Camp going home for
the day with fumes of
human roast clinging
rebelliously to his hairy
nostrils will stop
at the way-side sweet shop
and pick up a chocolate
for his tender offspring
waiting at home for Daddy's
return…

Praise bounteous
providence if you will
that grants even an ogre
a tiny glow-worm
tenderness encapsulated
in icy caverns of a cruel
heart or else despair
for in the very germ
of that kindred love is
lodged the perpetuity
of evil.

Chinua Achebe

EXAMINER'S HINTS

You will have studied both of these poems in advance of the exam and so you should have gained a good understanding of what they are about and the techniques their writers use. However, you won't know exactly what the question on the poetry anthology will be until you see the exam paper. It is, therefore, important that you read it carefully and decide exactly what it requires. Be careful to answer the question which is printed on the paper and not the one you hoped was printed there!

POETRY POST-1914

Question 3

Compare the ways the poets of *The send-off* and *The hero* write about soldiers involved in war.

[20 marks]

The send-off

Down the close darkening lanes they sang their way
To the siding-shed,
And lined the train with faces grimly gay.

Their breasts were stuck all white with wreath and spray
As men's are, dead.

Dull porters watched them and a casual tramp
Stood staring hard,
Sorry to miss them from the upland camp.

Then, unmoved, signals nodded, and a lamp
Winked to the guard.

So secretly, like wrongs hushed-up, they went.
They were not ours:
We never heard to which front these were sent;

Nor there if they yet mock what women meant
Who gave them flowers.

Shall they return to beating of great bells
In wild train loads?
A few, a few, too few for drums and yells,

May creep back, silent to village wells,
Up half-known roads.

Wilfred Owen

The hero

'Jack fell as he'd have wished,' the Mother said,
And folded up the letter that she'd read.
'The Colonel writes so nicely.' Something broke
In the tired voice that quavered to a choke.
She half looked up. 'We mothers are so proud
Of our dead soldiers.' Then her face was bowed.

Quietly the Brother Officer went out.
He'd told the poor old dear some gallant lies
That she would cherish all her days, no doubt.
For while he coughed and mumbled, her weak eyes
Had shone with gentle triumph, brimmed with joy,
Because he'd been so brave, her glorious boy.

He thought how 'Jack', cold-footed, useless swine,
Had panicked down the trench that night the mine
Went up at Wicked Corner; how he'd tried
To get sent home, and how, at last, he died,
Blown to small bits. And no one seemed to care
Except that lonely woman with white hair.

Siegfried Sassoon

EXAMINER'S HINTS

You will have studied these poems in preparation for your exam. You are being asked to write a comparison of the way different poets treat the same subject. You will gain high marks by showing a good understanding of the poets' feelings towards their subjects and of the way they use linguistic devices to convey them.

WRITING TO ANALYSE, REVIEW, COMMENT

Question 1

'This year it is nanotechnology; forty years ago it was nuclear power; no doubt some early man had doubts about the wheel.'

There are always concerns about any new advances in science and technology. Analyse and comment on some examples of such inventions and the concerns associated with them.   [20 marks]

EXAMINER'S HINTS

This task asks you to analyse information and to comment on it. Quite possibly, the exam paper will contain some stimulus material to help you to organise your ideas. I have given a suggested plan below for approaching this topic which can act as stimulus material. Examiners will be looking for a logically structured piece of writing which uses an objective tone to make judgements about the particular topics to which you refer.

SCIENCE AND TECHNOLOGY
Key discoveries

Electricity
- Natural resource
- What it's done to improve human living conditions
- It's allowed people to control their lives and not be subject to daylight, etc.
- Any real problems?

Computer technology
- Transformed our lives in less than 50 years
- List and comment on advantages
- What were the main fears?
- Is there a danger of computers taking over?

Internal combustion engine and flight
- Opened up travel opportunities
- Linked different parts of the world
- Dangers to life
- Pollution of environment

Nanotechnology
- Good example of the unknown
- Potential benefits
- Unforeseen dangers

Conclusion
- All discoveries have potentially dangerous side effects
- However, we tend to accept them and focus on benefits
- Once the knowledge is there it cannot be removed

WRITING TO INFORM, EXPLAIN, DESCRIBE

Question 2

Explain what you have learnt about yourself and others through playing games.

[20 marks]

EXAMINER'S HINTS

This is a writing task which requires you to inform and explain. It is important that you follow the instruction and write about yourself and your own experiences. You have a free choice as to how exactly you define the words 'playing games' but remember that the task requires you to explain what you have learnt about yourself and not to describe the games you enjoy playing.

WRITING TO ARGUE, PERSUADE, ADVISE

Question 3

'We all need some excitement and risk in our lives.'

Write the words of a speech in which you try to persuade members of your year group to agree with this point of view.

[20 marks]

EXAMINER'S HINTS

This task requires you to write to persuade and you should, therefore, choose your vocabulary carefully to make the most of emotive language. You should also think about using examples and references to support and reinforce your argument. Finally, note that you are being asked to write the words of a speech; it is important that you make some attempt to adopt an oral register and include some rhetorical devices in your answer. However, you should also try to avoid writing an over-colloquial response; this is, after all, a test of writing!

Non-fiction texts

Question 1

All the answers in this section are A/A* grade answers. The examiner's comments explain why they are very good answers. Compare your own answers with them and decide whether your answers contain all the features that are needed in order to achieve the top grade.

1

The three opinions in the article which I have chosen to write about are as follows:

"Prince Charles has warned that life on Earth could be wiped out by scientists 'playing God' with potentially lethal new technologies."

The first half of this statement is almost certainly a fact as it would be possible to check with newspaper reports, etc. whether Prince Charles did actually make this statement. However, what he is claimed to have said is certainly an opinion. This is indicated primarily by the vocabulary, as the article uses the conditional tense "could" which implies that what was said is speculation. The word "potentially" is also used and this too suggests that there is only a possibility that the Prince's fears may come true. Finally, there's the obvious point that as the technologies described have not yet been fully developed, no-one can know for sure whether these dangers will happen or not.

"The row follows claims by some experts that nanotechnology could spark a freak accident – the so-called 'grey goo' nightmare – where tiny nano-robots could gobble up the earth."

Again, this statement uses the word "could" twice and this implies that there is no absolute guarantee that such an outcome would occur. It is also stated that these are "claims" made by "some experts". "Claims" means that these ideas are unsupported speculations and not provable facts, and the fact that only some experts think this could happen (and these experts aren't named) is an indication that not all experts agree, which they would do if the comment could be proved as true.

"The idea of self-replicating nanorobots is pure science fiction."

This statement would seem to suggest that such a situation could never happen. Although there is no proof that it could, equally there is no absolute proof that it couldn't and so it must be an opinion rather than a fact. It is also worth noting that it was made by the Chief Executive of the Institute of Nanotechnology who would be likely to want to present a positive view of nanotechnology, and she also goes on to say that "you cannot regulate every aspect of nanotechnology", which would seem to contradict her earlier statement.

Examiner's comments

There are six marks available for this question which means that a maximum of two will be given for each example chosen. This answer **identifies three opinions** taken from the passage and **focuses clearly and economically on explaining** why they are so. The answer deals with both the **language** used (remember that a skilful writer can make opinions appear to be facts through choice of vocabulary) and with the **content** of the passage. It also shows an awareness of some of the **limitations of the writer's argument**. There is **precise and appropriate use of quotation and reference** and the points made in this way are thoroughly **explained and directly related to the task**.

2

Nanotechnology is a scientific process which is based on the use of incredibly small parts of matter – individual atoms and molecules – in order to make a wide range of materials. It was first thought of about 40 years ago when some scientists realised that the future was in the use of very small, rather than increasingly larger machines. It only really became a feasible option in 1990, by which time microscopes which were sufficiently powerful to study these miniscule forms had been produced. The process of nanotechnology allows scientists to manipulate (and alter) the fundamental basis of all living matter and already they have succeeded in producing extremely small microchips.

There are many potential advantages that can be gained from this process, particularly in medicine. For example, it is possible to produce tiny machines which can study the development of tumours from within and nanotechnology techniques can also be used to speed up the healing processes. It is also thought that it will be possible to make extremely light materials to be used in the manufacture of aircraft.

The most far-reaching claim for nanotechnology is that, within the next ten years, scientists will produce miniscule robots which will be able to assemble anything, atom by atom, to produce a perfect object. It is also thought that it will be possible to programme these "nanobots" to replicate themselves.

It is this point that gives the greatest cause for concern as some people fear that, if things go wrong, this replication could go on without stopping and that a mutant strain of billions of these robots could escape from the laboratory and, by feeding on whatever matter they find around them, consume the entire planet.

Examiner's comments

This response shows a very thorough **overall understanding** of the material. It selects many **details** from the passage, all of which are **specifically related to the question**. The student demonstrates her understanding by **re-ordering and synthesising points** – this shows that connections between different ideas have been fully taken on board. There is also good use of the student's **own words** and an attempt to expand on some points in order to make their **implications** clear. Finally, the student has **kept all strands of the question in focus** throughout, which helps to bind the answer together.

3

Both articles are about nanotechnology and both make the point that it is something which could have potential dangers, in particular the "grey goo" effect. The first article adopts a more sensational approach as is suggested by the language of its headline, "Nightmare of the Grey Goo", and this is continued by its opening which refers to Prince Charles's concerns that scientists may be "playing God" with "potentially lethal new technologies". By using such an important public figure as the heir to the throne, the writer of the article encourages his readers to question the wisdom of these scientists.

Throughout this article, the writer is adopting a negative approach to the subject of nanotechnology and most of the sources he refers to, such as Jonathon Porritt and Zac Goldsmith, are environmentalists who, not surprisingly, express their concerns about what might happen. Although the article makes some references to the possible beneficial effects of this technology, they are hidden away in the middle and described in language such as "miracle lightweight materials" which suggests that perhaps they are not to be taken too seriously. It should also be noted that those in favour of nanotechnology are described as "enthusiasts", which implies that they may have more enthusiasm than common sense, and that one of the people who is quoted as being in favour of nanotechnology is none other than the Prime Minister himself. The implication here is that, if the Prime Minister is in favour then perhaps we shouldn't really trust him, which is an attitude usually conveyed by the Mail on Sunday in which this article was printed.

The second article uses much less sensational language; rather than having science fiction suggestions in its headline it takes a much more balanced approach: "Tiny robots with massive potential". It is interesting to note that this is written by "A Mail on Sunday Reporter" rather than by a named writer. This article uses much more formal language and adopts a more informative approach. It explains the development of nanotechnology and supports this with facts and figures ("the concept will be a reality in just ten or 20 years"). These facts and the writer's generally balanced tone allow the readers to weigh up the points made in the article and to feel that they are being given reliable and correct information. Therefore, when the writer mentions what could be a serious danger resulting from nanotech experiments, the readers are prepared to take it seriously rather than to dismiss it as a piece of over-excitable journalism.

Examiner's comments

There are 10 marks available for this question and so there is no need to write at extreme length. However, it is important that you show a good grasp of the main similarities and differences between the two passages and can illustrate and explain these clearly.

This response shows a **sound overall understanding of the different ways the two articles deal with material on the same topic** and scores its marks in particular by the ways in which it comments on the way the first article uses references to individual figures to comment on and support its ideas. It also shows a good understanding of how the article is **aimed at a particular group of readers** with particular attitudes and there is good analysis of the writer's use of sensationalist language.

The contrast between the different approaches of the two articles is clearly shown by the way in which the student writes about the two headlines, and the **references to the writer's tone** in the second article is a perfectly valid response to the use of language.

4

Both articles are intended to make the readers question the values of nanotechnology and both use headlines which focus attention on the potential dangers which may arise from such research. In fact, both headlines sound as if they could be the titles of science fiction films although "Nightmare of the Grey Goo" suggests something more frightening and unknown than "Who will control the nanobots?" This science fiction nightmare approach is also conveyed by the photographs which accompany each article. The picture of the magnified ant which is at the head of the Grey Goo article is particularly scary and the ant appears as if it's some monster from outer space. The writer's clear intention here is to provoke a scared response in his readers with visions of giant ants taking over the world. This is a very effective way of influencing the readers' response to the article especially as nowhere does it make any reference to this in its content! Jonathon Porritt's article also has a photograph which looks like a spacecraft about to land but

is, in fact, an artist's impression of a tiny robot inside a human artery being used in medical research.

The writers of the articles express their concerns over nanotechnology in slightly different ways. The author of the Grey Goo passage is clearly setting out to make his readers take a negative approach to the research he describes. He quotes from people concerned with the environment (including Prince Charles), all of whom express serious concerns about what may happen. The implication here is that all of these experts know more about the dangers of what may happen than do the politicians and enthusiasts who are in favour of the research. The writer quite cleverly builds up the suggestion that there is a conspiracy on behalf of governments and institutes of nanotechnology to keep the potential dangers a secret. Another way he does this is by stating that the Americans are likely to use the technology to develop weapons for defence purposes.

The language used in the Grey Goo article is deliberately chosen to provoke an emotional response from its readers with words and phrases such as "wiped out", "grey goo catastrophe", "meddling with molecules" (the use of alliteration here helps to emphasise the point), "freak accident", "nightmare" and "gobble up the Earth". The effect of this vocabulary is to create a tone of fear and threat and it results in the readers questioning the motives of those who engage in research into nanotechnology and prejudices them against such research.

Jonathon Porritt, who is quoted in the Grey Goo article, nevertheless adopts a more reasoned and balanced approach in his own article. He begins by bringing in his personal response; he tries to explain what nanotechnology involves and emphasises that, as yet, we don't know its full potential: "Some people see it as the most important breakthrough since the wheel; others believe it threatens the end of life as we know it." He appears to be rather sceptical of the claims made about nanotechnology as he talks about "a classic bit of nanohype" and he refers to nanobots whizzing around cleaning up pollution as if they're some kind of child's toy, but, on the other hand, he also refers to those who question nanotech's potential as "prophets of doom", which suggests he is not fully in support of their attitude either.

Porritt, in general, appears to be presenting an honest evaluation of his own feelings and this is very effectively conveyed in his short, sharp statement which follows quite a long sentence questioning whether we should support or oppose nanotech scientists, "I haven't a clue." This is a very effective use of a colloquial statement and encourages the reader to share the writer's concerns but in the same balanced way that Porritt has expressed them. It would be a shame to lose the possible benefits of nanotechnology, he says, although we must be aware of its potential dangers. The writer's suggestion that we should "proceed with a great deal more caution and forethought than is currently the case" is a logical conclusion expressed in a balanced and reasonable tone and successfully encourages the readers to share his point of view without scaring them into it with tales of global disaster.

Examiner's comments

This is a **thorough and detailed response** which shows a clear awareness of the differences between the two passages. It also explains the methods used by both writers to persuade us to share their viewpoint and **concludes with a judgement** on which has been more successful.

The answer shows a good understanding of the ways in which the photographs are used to enhance the content of the articles and also explains this clearly; it is important to remember that with this type of question, explaining **how and why** writers achieve particular results is central to scoring high marks. The answer **focuses on relevant details** of the writers' arguments, **paraphrases them to show understanding** and also shows a **perceptive appreciation of the vocabulary and register** used in the articles and how this is part of the writers' method of persuading their readers to share their points of view.

Poems from different cultures

Question 2

Both poems are about living creatures and both are about living creatures which are generally considered to be unattractive, unpleasant and dangerous. Nissim Ezekiel's poem is about a scorpion and recalls an incident in his childhood when his mother was stung by one. Chinua Achebe writes about vultures which are also unpleasant carrion creatures.

Both poets begin by describing the weather which provides a background to the events. In Ezekiel's poem, the scorpion had been driven to seek shelter in their house as a result of the heavy rain; the setting for Achebe's poem is the "greyness and drizzle" of "one despondent dawn". The ways in which the poets treat the setting is indicative of their differing treatment of their subject matter. Ezekiel deals with a domestic incident; his mother is stung by accident and the poet uses this incident and its aftermath to illustrate the responses such an incident provokes from a range of people. Achebe is concerned with making a wider point

about the nature of evil and its existence in the world. In his poem, the vultures are seen as part of the generally threatening nature of the universe; Ezekiel focuses on the general limitations of human behaviour.

Ezekiel describes the scorpion as "the evil one" which has come into the poet's home; the idea of it being like the devil is reinforced by the description of its tail as "diabolic". This tail flashes in the dark room and stings the poet's mother; the peasants of the village come in buzzing like a swarm of flies (the simile suggests that perhaps to the poet's family they are an unwanted irritation) and pray to God to paralyse the evil one. The poem then continues to present a vividly dramatic picture of the scene in the hut. Now that the scorpion has done its deed, it is no longer a central figure in the drama.

In contrast to the frantic human activity being described in Ezekiel's poem, Achebe focuses in an almost objective way on the activity of the vultures. They are sitting on a "dead tree"; the male vulture's head is described as "bashed-in" and like a pebble. The birds' eating habits are described in bald detail, "picked the eyes of a swollen corpse…ate the things in its bowel", after which they are "gorged". There is nothing poetic or attractive about these creatures and yet the male is described as inclining "affectionately" towards his mate and the poet comments how strange it is for love to "pick a corner in that charnel-house".

This observation is extended to a comment on human nature. Even the Commandant at Belsen, says Achebe, must have had some human feelings for his own family: after a day burning the flesh of his victims (the impersonal cruelty of the vultures is used to emphasise the inhuman attitude of the Nazis) he would stop to buy chocolate for his children on his way home. Achebe admits that he is unsure what this reflection means; does the affection of the vultures and the parental love of the Commandant indicate that love can be found even in the midst of evil or does it simply suggest that love and evil are inseparable and that the latter grows within love? This comment and the tone of the poem as a whole leave the reader questioning whether there is any divine influence on our lives at all or whether the universe is simply indifferent towards us.

In its own way, Ezekiel's poem raises similar considerations. The evil scorpion has done its deed and the eager villagers are each suggesting their own remedy to deal with it. They appear to be relishing the excitement of the incident and pass on much of their local wisdom to the mother, for example, "may the poison purify your flesh of desire, and your spirit of ambition, they said". The poet repeats the phrase "they said" in order to emphasise the ritualistic way in which the peasants are speaking. Although the poet's mother is in the centre of all this attention, there is very little mention of her in this part of the poem. All the attention is on the villagers going about their ritual and the implication is that they are more concerned with the opportunity the situation gives them for moralising than for the victim herself.

In fact, we are given the impression that the mother's suffering provides the villagers with an opportunity to escape from their mundane lives. More candles, neighbours and insects arrive as the mother twists in agony "groaning on a mat". Her husband, despite his scepticism about superstition, tries every curse and remedy he can think of. Finally, he tries to purify the poison by pouring paraffin on the mother's toe and lighting it. Only at the end of the poem does attention turn to the mother herself whose main concern is for others: "Thank God the scorpion picked on me and spared my children" – her quiet love for her family contrasts with the bustle and activity of the main part of the poem.

Both poems reflect the different cultures of their authors in their setting and background. Neither poem uses rhyme and both are written in a form of free verse which allows a clear and precise picture of the different episodes to be built up in the readers' minds. Achebe's poem, in particular, conveys the harsh indifference of the vultures and what they represent through his choice of words such as "broken bone of a dead tree", "bashed-in head" and "icy caverns of a cruel heart". Ezekiel uses repetition effectively to get across the urgency in the room as the mother twists and groans in pain.

Both poems, while on the surface dealing with living creatures, also address themes and issues which are universal. Achebe writes about the way in which positive human emotions (family love) can still be present even among those responsible for the most appalling acts of human cruelty; the vultures are ugly, unattractive creatures who with no compunction feed off the corpse they have found in a ditch, but nevertheless show what appears to be affection for each other. The poet uses them to represent symbolically the actions of human beings who practise genocide – something just as relevant to Achebe's Africa as it was to Second World War Europe. The objective tone of his poem allows the readers to draw their own moral from the episode and his closing lines emphasise the ambivalence of his feelings:

> "Praise bounteous
> providence if you will
> that grants even an ogre
> a tiny glow-worm
> tenderness encapsulated
> in icy caverns of a cruel
> heart or else despair
> for in the very germ
> of that kindred love is
> lodged the perpetuity
> of evil."

We are left wondering whether love can redeem evil or whether the "perpetuity of evil" in some way derives from love; the tone of the poem would perhaps suggest that the latter view is more probable.

On the other hand, Ezekiel uses the scorpion to represent the unpredictable presence of evil in the world and the reactions of the villagers and the poet's father reveal how limited our knowledge is in dealing with it. The conclusion of his poem, however, which focuses on the natural love and concern of a mother for her children, suggests a more positive feeling about human nature than the rather bleak attitude suggested by Achebe:

> "My mother only said
> Thank God the scorpion picked on me
> and spared my children."

Both poets, therefore, through dealing with incidents specific to their own cultures use living creatures to make us reflect on the more universal issues of human nature and the relationship between love and evil in our lives.

Examiner's comments

This is a **full and detailed** answer which deals thoughtfully with the texts, **selecting and highlighting key points** on which to comment. It shows **good appreciation of the writer's attitudes and ideas and quotes appropriately** to support its arguments. There is also a **very clear awareness of the wider issues** which both poems deal with and there is a **clear awareness of the need to make consistent comparisons and contrasts** between the two poems. There is also a good understanding of the ways in which the poets have used **language** to create their effects.

Poetry post-1914

Question 3

Although both poems are concerned with soldiers fighting in the First World War, the poets approach their subject in different ways. Wilfred Owen describes a group of soldiers as they are about to leave their camp in England for the trenches. Sassoon's poem describes the scene when a mother is informed that her son has been killed in battle. What links the two poems is the writers' attitude towards war; both are angry about the unnecessary waste of young lives and also about the hypocritical attitude which those in important positions adopt towards those they send to their deaths. Both poets show pity for the young soldiers and succeed in conveying this very forcefully to their readers.

Owen's poem is set at night; the recruits sing their way through "close darkening lanes" as they make their way to the "siding-shed". The alliteration of the letter "s" makes it sound as if someone is whispering and that the whole episode is some kind of conspiracy. The soldiers wait to board the train with "faces grimly gay" and the oxymoron in the last two words again hints at something unnatural taking place. The soldiers have been decorated with flowers but the poet compares them to the wreaths placed on dead bodies and again alerts the reader to the likely fate of these men. Owen continues to create the impression that there is something secret and shameful about the way these men are being packed off to war. The only person likely to miss them is a tramp and the only other people present are the "dull porters" who watch them – almost with the suggestion that they are there to prevent them from escaping. The sense of conspiracy is increased when Owen personifies the signals nodding and the lamps winking; both of these objects seem to know more about the soldiers' fate than they do themselves. There is a phrase in the fifth stanza which perfectly sums up the attitude of the authorities towards these men; they leave secretly, "like wrongs hushed-up". This is followed by the blunt statement, emphasised by being a single, short line, "They were not ours". Nobody, it seems, wants to take responsibility for these men or for what may happen to them. Up to this point the poet's attitude has not been fully clear. Has he been writing as a detached observer or as one who feels pity for the soldiers? In the final stanzas his sense of pity is clearly conveyed. It is clear to him that these recruits are being sent to their deaths and it is too much to hope that they will return "to beating of great bells". Only a very few are likely to survive the war and those who do will "creep" back (the air of secrecy is being sustained) and they will have been so changed by their experience that they will only half know where they are going.

Owen famously said that his subject was war and the pity of war, "the poetry is in the pity". In this poem in a quiet, ironic and understated way he conveys this sense of pity very powerfully.

Sassoon also uses irony in his poem but in a much more savage way than Owen. The title of the poem is itself ironic as we learn that Jack, in fact, did not die a hero's death and that the officers had very little respect for him. The poem is written in three six line stanzas which rhyme aa bb cc, etc. This plain and simple format is very effective as it suggests both the naivety of the mother and the cynical attitude of the officer who brings her the news of her son's death.

The poet very skilfully controls the reader's responses. At the beginning of the poem the mother receives the news of her son's death in a letter so nicely written by the Colonel. "Jack fell as he'd have wished". The mother's comment about being "so proud of our dead soldiers" indicates that she has been convinced by the propaganda put out by those who control the war and does not know anything about the true conditions in the trenches.

In the second stanza, however, we are allowed an insight into the mind of the Brother Officer who appears to embody the attitude of those nameless and faceless characters responsible for sending Owen's soldiers off to war. He is scornful towards the mother, "the poor old dear" to whom he'd told the lies she wished to hear about the death of her "glorious boy". Far from being a hero, Jack had proved to be a "cold-footed, useless swine" who panicked and was unheroically "blown to small bits". Not one of his colleagues seemed to care and the only person to grieve would be "that lonely woman with white hair". This line reminds us that the son's death has left his mother alone in her old age. By the end of the poem, Sassoon's anger has become clearly established. The reader does not care that the son has died unheroically but rather is bitter at the hypocrisy of the officers and of the whole system which is ashamed to admit to the lies it tells the population about the glories of the war to which it is sending them to be slaughtered.

Together, these two poems present a powerful criticism of the system which allows such things to happen, and between them deal with the complete cycle of the fate of many young men involved in the First World War. Owen's poem describes the recruits leaving for the front; Sassoon's presents the all too familiar scene of a mother being informed of the death of her soldier son. What links the two poems in their treatment of war is the poets' anger and bitterness at the hypocrisy of those responsible for sending so many men to their deaths by making them believe that war is something heroic and glorious. Both Owen and Sassoon were directly involved in the fighting in the trenches and they were committed to describing the war as it really was rather than to going along with the official propaganda; their attitude did much to influence the attitudes of later generations.

Examiner's comments

This is a very **detailed response** which shows a perceptive appreciation of the poets' techniques and which makes **consistently relevant and thoughtful comparisons** between the poems. There is a **close textual analysis**, particularly of the Owen poem, and the student shows a good appreciation of the way the poets use words to influence the reader's response. The student also shows a **good knowledge of figures of speech** such as alliteration and oxymoron but, more importantly, is able to **explain how they are used to create a particular effect**. The student has clearly responded strongly to the poems and this answer shows evidence of a **convincing and sincere personal response.**

Writing to analyse, review, comment

Question 1

It is human nature to be curious and to want to know how things work. Throughout history this has led to mankind inventing and discovering many things which, in the long run, have proved beneficial to our lives. Nearly all of these discoveries have the potential to be used for good or ill. In this essay I shall consider a few of them and assess their value to our lives.

First of all, let us consider electricity. This is something which we take for granted. When we watch television, use the computer or take a shower we don't really think about what gives these things the power to work. It's electricity, it's there and we use it. However, it's only during the last 200 or so years that mankind has had this privilege. Before the discovery that the power of electricity (which is a natural force) could be controlled, people's lives were much different. Without artificial light the working day was controlled by the hours of daylight; people went to bed and got up as the sun set and rose. Without the understanding of electricity, even highly civilised people like the ancient Romans could not make the most of their knowledge.

Of course, not all uses of electricity are good; timers used to detonate bombs and other devices also rely on it but very few people now would want electricity banned as its good points far outweigh the bad.

The same could be said for the invention of computers. Within half a century our lives have been totally transformed by these machines and it is not necessary to repeat all the advantages they offer. However, when they were first being developed many people expressed fears about them. They felt that they would make us too dependent on them, that we would become lazy and that computers would take over the world. That hasn't happened. Computers are widely used and are essential to the smooth running of businesses, transport systems and to education. The internet has opened up a wealth of information which is readily accessible and e-mail has revolutionised communications. Admittedly, there are websites which contain obscene and violent material and it can be argued that some people, especially teenage boys, waste much of their time playing computer games but, overall, these are minor limitations and very few people would deny the importance of computers to our lives.

Transport and travel have been considerably improved by the invention of the internal combustion engine which led to the invention of the car and the aeroplane. Although these machines have some problems connected to them such as the risks attached to human life in using them and the fact that the fumes and noise they produce are adding to the pollution of the environment, nevertheless they are an integral part of our lives and we would find it very difficult to live without them.

And now, some scientists are expressing concerns about the developments of nanotechnology. These concerns are, no doubt, very similar to those expressed when computers, electricity and cars were first being developed. It is right that these worries should be made public so that they can be looked into. However, it also appears that nanotechnology offers some potentially very exciting opportunities and it is almost certain that scientists will work on developing those and let the more dangerous side effects take care of themselves. Our experience over the centuries has shown that it is human nature to investigate and discover new things; once a piece of knowledge is in the human mind it cannot be removed and no-one would want to stand in the way of progress.

Examiner's comments

This is a **well-constructed and clearly expressed** piece of writing. It successfully analyses some examples of technological development and makes some excellent comments about them. It **begins with a direct statement** which immediately engages the reader. There is a **logical development through well-linked paragraphs** and the essay concludes by reinforcing the statement with which it opens. The student's vocabulary is well-chosen and well-suited to the purpose and there is a skilfully controlled **range of sentence structures and types**. The conclusion is a little hurried as time was obviously getting tight. However, overall this is a **maturely argued, detailed piece of writing** and deserves a top grade mark.

Writing to inform, explain, describe

Question 2

As a child I was lucky to have a vivid imagination. As my much older siblings had left home I was mostly left to my own devices (aided by a treasure trove of wonderful toys) to amuse myself, and enjoyed being alone. With the introduction of a play-group into my day, I was forced to interact with other children – a pastime I came to thoroughly enjoy, and something I often blame for my desire to constantly socialise instead of study...

I am a strong believer that the environment one is brought up in, and how one is introduced to pleasure and pain (and subsequently ways of dealing with both) is crucial to emotional evolution. For example, if a child is kept in isolation, he or she will be unable to interact naturally with peers, and quite possibly develop social problems later in life. Basic lessons like personal space and sharing are taught very early on in one's life, and are vital skills for the rest of one's existence.

As a result of my upbringing, I have evolved into someone who loves to be surrounded by people, a good communicator, but someone who highly values solitude. I get crowded very easily, and sometimes need to be able to disappear. I have learnt this over time, mostly through playing and interacting with other children.

"Play time", I find, always brings out people's true characters. Whether seven or seventeen, certain traits are always exposed when the need for team-work arises. For example, not everyone's a team-player, and the person with a hidden agenda stands out a mile when unity is needed. Programmes like "Big Brother" are interesting on this subject, as the contestants are needed to play as a team half of the time, and as driven individuals for the rest of it. It erases most of the scope for falsities, and encourages raw character analysis.

I remember a very old friend of mine once had an Easter egg hunt in her garden. It was boys against girls, and the person with the most eggs overall would also get a special prize. It was interesting to observe the ways in which the different sexes dealt with the task. The girls decided to all get as many as they could individually, and then choose someone to "win" and each give them half their eggs. The victor would in return share their prize amongst the team. The boys, however, started tearing around, each man for himself, shoving and pushing – competing right from the word "go". I can't remember who won, but it really showed up the differences between boys and girls.

I always think games, in whichever guise they appear, should remain a vital part of one's life. Role-playing and team efforts help us to understand ourselves and each other, and provide a little light relief from playschool, GCSEs, University or a job. Don't tell anyone, but I still pretend to be different people all the time. Sometimes I'm Ella, an art student from Sydney who collects curtains; sometimes I'm Ruby from New York who's 19 and is married to a fifty year old sugar daddy; or Esperanza, a Spanish gymnast who is running away from her ex-boyfriend who's just got out of prison. Don't laugh at me! These weird and wonderful characters let me totally step back from myself, and unravel my psyche from the complications of being almost sixteen. I also love the different reactions I get from people when I tell them my story, and the greatest challenge of all is trying to get them to believe some of my wilder concoctions.

You may now think I am a mentally unbalanced danger to the community, or simply a teenager who still enjoys being seven, and doesn't want to let go of her childhood. I'll leave it up to you to decide which is closer to the truth.

Examiner's comments

This is a **detailed, original and fully appropriate response** to the task. There is a **clear attempt to answer the question** and the student has selected episodes from her own experience on which to base her explanation of how playing games has taught her to understand herself. She makes this interesting by showing a **continued awareness of the reader** and, at times, addressing the reader directly. This is particularly well done in the concluding passage as the writer is clearly aware of **the importance of leaving a strong final impression in the reader's mind.** The writer has a wide vocabulary and is especially strong at using abstract terms which are important to this type of topic. However, these are balanced by **a quiet but effective tone** which adds to the appeal of the writing.

Writing to argue, persuade, advise

Question 3

In ancient times, when man was at his "manliest"(!), we did not believe in such nonsensical things as laws and rules! Our raw, natural impulses had freedom of speech. This basic, "primal" instinct remains within us, even today, albeit suppressed by the restrictions of society: the instinct to seek danger – to take risks. By taking risks, we experience excitement, and by overcoming them, we feel satisfaction! It is by introducing risk, and creating a challenge, that we are truly satisfied. As J F Kennedy once said – "We choose to go to the moon – not because it is easy, but because it is hard." What is life without that underlying element of risk? Why is it that such pursuits as drinking, smoking and taking drugs are so much more exciting when they are illegal? It is due to the "buzz" and exhilaration of defying rules, taking chances and going against the grain. Another famous quote reminds us to "never forget that only dead fish swim with the stream".

Therefore, I believe that we do all need excitement and risk in our lives. The dawn of this new "cyber-era" has modernised life to such an extent that our lives have become too restrained, too predictable. However, our ancient instinct for danger remains intact. We have started to find ways of venting our desires through "extreme sports" – what is the appeal of bungee-jumping and kayaking? It is the thrill of confronting danger and overcoming it. Similarly, what is the fun in a rollercoaster which turns you upside down? Or a 50 foot waterslide? Once again, it is the simulation of danger. We have managed to elude society's restricting grasp. However, our forefathers would laugh at the complexity of the methods we have employed to recreate emotions which they could experience so easily.

Another form of escape has recently appeared to us – through the idea of "virtuality". We can now vicariously carry out dangerous acts through a computer character! If we can't jump off cliffs, shoot people and drive fast cars, why not experience these "electric" experiences electronically? In the words of Max Frisch,

"Technology is a way of understanding the universe without having to experience it ourselves."

In the same way, action films and adventure novels appeal to us – due to the recreation of danger and the thrills of risk. Our favourite heroes and cartoon characters were daring – for example, Odysseus – a gambler, or Superman – a daredevil. Tales of daring exploits always excite the imagination.

However, we have regressed into a society in which too much is provided for – trapped in an urban jungle, we have almost forgotten the thrills that nature can provide. "Progress was alright but it has gone on for too long," said Ogden Nash. Nowadays, we are drifting into dreariness, ignorant and unaware of the escapes or risk. For us, risks include wearing "unstylish clothes" or buying shares (once again – an example of our natural instincts to gamble). For me, our ability to lull into this somnambulant state is the greatest risk of all. Unpredictability and risk enhance all our emotions and provide the greatest excitement possible. I, therefore, urge you to agree with me that we all need risk and danger in our lives.

Examiner's comments

This is a very **forceful, controlled piece of persuasive writing.** The student has sustained a **convincing oral register** throughout and, in particular, has made good use of **rhetorical questions, examples and quotations to reinforce his arguments.** There is a **consistent awareness of the reader** and vocabulary has been carefully chosen to persuade and convince. There is a **good use of humour** and a very effective **mix of long and short sentences to keep the reader's interest.** The **opening immediately creates interest** and the argument builds up to a **convincing conclusion** which also contains a final reminder that this is a speech and that the audience are being persuaded to agree with its ideas.